REBUILDING IN-PERSON WORSHIP

CATHY TOWNLEY

REBUILDING IN-PERSON WORSHIP

Overcoming Institutionalism
to Rewrite the Story
of Your Church's Future

Nashville

REBUILDING IN-PERSON WORSHIP:
OVERCOMING INSTITUTIONALISM TO REWRITE THE STORY OF YOUR CHURCH'S FUTURE

ISBN: 978-1-7910-4211-0

MANUFACTURED IN THE UNITED STATES OF AMERICA

CONTENTS

Part I:
Inside Your Building

Part II:
Outside Your Building

Part III:
Inside and Outside Your Building

Preface

WRITING YOUR OWN ENDING

Spoiler alert! I'm going to tell you how this book ends in the following sentence.

You're going to start working through the material in this book enthusiastically, then want to quit.

That's because of your church's changing realities and your uncertainty about how to turn things around. You're hoping this book is a miracle cure for your worship woes. When you find out it isn't and begin to see what you really must do to make worship changes that matter, your hope will falter. You'll need a pep talk to keep going. You'll find plenty of encouragement in these pages. But you'll have to keep reading and doing the work to receive them. Patience isn't your strong suit.

This Material's Point of View

The spoiler describes the angst of most churches that I have encountered during my 3.5 decades of leading worship, starting churches and worship services, consulting and coaching in nearly all mainline denominations, writing, teaching, and speaking about worship in various denominational gatherings. Worship is a sore spot because you have:

- experienced a decline, which showed up mostly in worship;
- looked for an easy solution to stop the bleeding, though not necessarily to grow;
- added new music or technology to an existing service;
- fought the worship wars because no one likes everything you did;
- threw together a new service and advertised on social media;
- expected new people to appear, but they didn't, so you ended the new service;
- promised your people the new people would appear if you did all the right stuff;
- suffered the anger and mistrust of your people because you broke your promise;

- heard about another new trend that will appeal to young people; or
- stopped caring about in-person worship in favor of the next quick fix.

How institutionalism predicts an unhappy ending to your church's story

The prologue depicts the impact of institutionalism upon worship development in local churches. Keeping the church's doors open is the primary motivation for churches that have experienced decline, especially those with an average worship attendance of under 100. When institutions are motivated by self-preservation, they lose touch with the people they exist to serve. Tiny and often ingrown churches can have little interest in engaging new people with the church and Christianity. That's the earmark of the toxic church.

For churches that want to grow, it's common to feel that if they do all the right things, all the new people will come to them. Or at least that's what the pastor has promised his or her members. So when that doesn't come to fruition, the church faces a bigger problem: mistrust. Even larger churches, with up to 250 in worship attendance, adopt that mantra: We must change our music and spend a lot of money on technology because that's what will matter to the new people. That's still institutionalism because it's wrapped around the expectation that new people will come to you, and that you can get them with your coolness. Leaders who have upgraded often say to me, "We get one new guest unit per week because of our new stuff." One? How representative is that unit of the emerging mission field outside your church's doors that will never walk in?

Worship has become a tool in most churches, either subtly or overtly. Why would a new person be drawn to a tool? Not even your members are. We all know the unhappy ending to this sad story.

Why and how to rebuild worship to rewrite your story's ending

In this book, we're targeting churches with worship attendance under 250. If your church has a worship attendance over 250, this material can still be useful. I work with larger churches that come to me to fix a new service that's dying. It doesn't take long to identify missed steps. We follow the same process laid out in these pages to turn things around, and in so doing, the lead pastor inevitably learns invaluable lessons that help him or her further develop worship through outreach rather than attraction. That's the hurdle for a large church: getting past their ability to attract new people by virtue of their size. Churched people in your area have heard of the larger churches. When Christians are looking for a new church, they're inclined to find their way to the church that's known. That's a problem smaller churches don't have: a reputation! But larger churches don't face the drama of resource constraints that smaller churches do. Leaders in smaller churches have to take on much of the work themselves to reverse their decline, whereas larger churches can hire or appoint a leader to address worship growth. Most of the examples and references in this material will come from the smaller churches I've worked with, so they can see what's possible for them specifically.

When churches between 100 and 250 reach out to me for worship guidance, it's usually to find a fix for a contemporary service that's languishing. Churches with fewer than 100 weekly worship participants typically have only one service. In many of these conversations, leaders are understandably hoping for a quick fix—a single change that will turn things around. But what will work is really seeking a path to genuine, lasting transformation. Worship decline is systemic. Surface-level adjustments rarely address its root causes. Once you understand the system, real and lasting growth becomes possible and you won't be as drawn to the quick fix illusion.

You can't effectively turn your church around from decline to growth by allowing the motivation of keeping your doors open to direct your actions. You will inevitably try to start from where you are, which implies finding the right sized band-aid for your worship wounds. Declining churches, or declining worship services, must start over if they want worship to be what it's intended to be: central to the Christian faith and the place we go to be in God's presence as a community. That would be a thriving faith community. You have enough people to feel alive, and more are connecting with your church and considering becoming part of it. You may indeed have had to upgrade your music and technology and learn a few things. But you're not relying on those things to reach the curious seeker who hasn't yet connected with faith. Instead, you pursue faith beyond church walls. You learn to tell your faith story and build transformational relationships with those who aren't connected with the church, to introduce them to Jesus. You don't have to meet anyone new. You already know people who fit that description. You only need to learn to be you: a Christ follower who is serious about following Jesus, where Jesus is trying to lead you: into the mission field.

The Prequel That Clarifies This Moment in Time

The journey you'll take to make worship the kind of environment that honors God

Worship transforms when it's built upon faith development, and faith development matures when Christians become disciples who make disciples. When you learn to talk about faith as a regular part of everyday life, you return to the public gathering with gratitude because you have been hearing your own voice utter faith. How many people in your faith community gather on Sunday morning because they're grateful, in your estimation?

When you pursue faith development beyond the church walls, new people become interested in your church. But believe it or not, that's not really the point of moving into this way of thinking and being a Christian who is part of a faith community that's trying to grow. The fact is that in-person worship changes when you tell your faith story repeatedly. You—the one who is doing the telling—want to return to the public gathering because you wish to honor God for your very existence. Your expectations of the public gathering have changed, and so have your public expressions. You wouldn't be able to live with a worship gathering that's not expressive. How expressive is your gathering now?

If one of the people you're discipling joins you in the public gathering one day, God might indeed use your public praise to influence your guest toward faith. God does that. Worship is God's deal. We show up to it because God is really there in ways we don't see elsewhere in the faith community. But we're not really thinking about what God will do through us with our guest. We're not trying to be the cool church. We're just trying to be us. The rest is up to God.

The worship service is now a very new and powerful place in your church.

The author's backstory: Why this focus? Why now?

For a church to reach the place of authentic power in the public gathering, it will require a first step: getting past the cynicism about it. The church has grown cynical about public worship. There is a subtle belief afoot that new people won't participate, so why bother? New people do want to experience worship. Not all, but some. It's the church's job to reach out to find those who do. To remain mistrusting is to put up your own roadblock.

I confess I've been cynical about those who were cynical! After decades of coaching and teaching and seeing the same mistakes repeatedly, I was convinced that hardly any leaders would ever be willing to do what it would take to transform worship in their churches. So I distanced myself from my work.

And God let me, until God didn't. God started bringing me people who wanted to change worship, even when I had practically retired to pursue my golf game and spend time with my granddaughter. I knew that if I didn't impart some seriously more profound teaching to the various new clients, their projects would fail. I had to get back to writing. I fought it. I have a folder on my computer labeled *"Seriously? Another new book?"*

In the process of writing and rewriting my thoughts and experiences about worship and worship growth, I realized my disgruntlement was misguided. Please accept my deepest apologies! As I wrote, I realized it was I who was the bigger problem—my attitude and the way I was trying to communicate the connection between worship and outreach. Writing all of this has been a several-year journey to find a way to help leaders put it all together. The more I wrote, the more I understood that God had people out there who were ready to rebuild worship. We're all in the same boat: It's our job to allow God to lead us to finding those who are prepared for the message of hope in Jesus. God is preparing them. So I'm saying yes to God now.

The conflict of the learning curve that prefers quick fixes

Perhaps you've noticed the literary or story language in titles and headings so far. This is a storybook first and foremost, so the use of story or literary language provides additional insight into the journey you'll be on if you decide to take it!

Backstories, conflicts, and denouements, or turning points, are your key words for rewriting the story of your church's future from decline to growth.

The backstory of your church is its decline and the reasons for it. The conflict is that you need a system to bring a local church along in this process. If any reader were pursuing faith sharing on their own, they wouldn't need a system. You could do this alone, and it would be a valid approach. But you're probably not doing this alone.

The organizational approach to outreach is church planting, which now makes your steep learning curve even steeper. The church-planting structure revolves around telling others about Jesus, but it is a numerical addition to the mix. Reaching benchmarks accelerates your faith-sharing process. But it's demanding, and you're going to fight it.

There's more conflict. Infusing church-planting behaviors into the faith community so you can continue to share your faith and impact your territory, enabling in-person worship to thrive and grow more, is ongoing in a leader's and a church's life. Come to terms with that in a nano-second.

Denouement

There will be several turning points in your pursuit. But change remains slow and incremental. One turning point will be in accepting that. Changing worship through church-planting practices takes about nine to eighteen months the first time. You'll get a boost from it, but it's not enough if you want to produce actual culture change in your church.

If your church membership is under 100, you'll try to get everyone on board. That approach usually backfires, as people want to know why they need to give up worship as it is now. You must be willing to target and start with just a handful of people exploring the basics of prayer and the connection to faith sharing beyond church walls. It will change you to do that.

Leaders of churches with 100–250 members often start by trying to engage their board because they think they need awareness of the key leaders and maybe permission to set up this "new program." There's a preferred time to introduce board members to new ways of thinking about worship through faith sharing, but it's typically not at the front end of this work. No one needs permission from a hierarchy or management group to learn how to follow God by sharing faith. Taking charge of your own life to pursue Jesus in depth is transformational.

Focusing on the 20 percent

Willingness to focus on a smaller group that's ready for change is a readiness marker for a leader, and for some members who worry that their friends might not be part of your outreach focus. Those who agree to become disciples who make disciples will comprise roughly 20–30 percent of your worship attendance. Rebuilding in-person worship requires that you strategically gather a small group of people and focus your attention on them from the start. That group might be only 10–12 percent of worship attendance. It will grow to about 20 percent or so. You can help all your members understand that you're becoming a faith-sharing church. In fact, doing so supports outreach efforts. But don't get distracted trying to bring the resistors along by teaching faith sharing to everyone. It won't take root, and it will harm the process. Give the 20 percent more attention than the rest of the body from the start. Doing so will impact your schedule, your communication, and maybe your stress level! We deal with all of that in the coming pages.

Doing so will also impact the way you use training materials. Churches I'm working with often reveal that they're using my material and other material that seems similar. Most existing resources on discipleship focus on the internal church, not on learning a faith testimony to get you outside the church. The 20–30 percent don't need basic discipleship training. They are already growing more serious about their faith journey, which is why they want to take faith to a new level by becoming a disciple-making disciple. They most need to learn how to articulate their faith in everyday language for everyday conversations, which this material provides.

You may need more basic training for the larger part of the body, and some other discipleship materials may help you do that. That gives you two groups: a large group (the 80 percent) and the smaller group (the 20 percent). Most smaller churches are more comfortable trying to garner the attention of the 80 percent. This material moves you into a different value system.

Developing Your Story's Plotline

Here's the recommended approach for pursuing this book:

- The leader recognizes it's time for a change in worship development.
- The leader reviews this material and prays to include a handful of members or constituents on the journey, based on the participant's desire to grow in faith.
- You'll teach members things about worship to deepen their understanding of the public gathering.
- You'll do all this in a timeline you establish while reading the material.
- You'll discern if you want to move into the church-planting applications for worship development at the end of part I.
- If you continue into part II at the end of part I, then it's time to engage your board in some bigger decisions.

Below is an annotated journey through this material, chapter by chapter.

Part I: Inside Your Building

Lay groundwork for faith sharing and worship development to take root through learning about worship and developing your personal faith story. You won't be doing actual faith sharing beyond church walls yet. Part I helps you change your mind about worship and discern whether you're going to take the next step of faith sharing beyond church walls by preparing you for it.

- *Discerning Your Role.* All church leaders must find a way to absorb this material, even if they don't lead a study with their people.
- *Leading Worship.* Recognizing the different ways God "behaves" in the public gathering is key to rebuilding in-person worship.

- *Expecting Pushback.* Resistance to faith sharing and worship changes is a given. But where does it come from, and how do you navigate it?
- *Getting Comfortable with Faith Talk.* Learn, write, and share your testimony!
- *Doing the Math.* Come to terms with growth formulae. This chapter is likely to offend you.
- *Countering Culture.* How can we utilize culture to remain countercultural?

Part I chapter organization:

- Chapter Notes—suggestions for how to absorb the material, followed by
    - a *Chapter Notes* reflection question to answer
- I. Real-life Coaching Stories—true stories from my ministry, followed by
    - some *Coaching Stories* reflection questions to answer.
- II. Backstories of Institutionalism—how we got here, followed by
    - some *Backstories* reflection questions to answer.
- III. Rewriting Your Church's Story—steps toward change, followed by
    - *Rewrite Your Story* reflection questions to answer.

Part II: Outside Your Building

You'll begin your journey into the mission field to share faith and grow your faith community. You've laid the groundwork in part I through story development. It has helped you change your mind about worship. Now you're changing your behavior. You're adding pace, as well as church-planting language and strategies. You'll notice the shift, even though you won't eliminate the impact of storytelling on your behavior.

- Phase One: *Lay Groundwork (Behind Closed Doors).* You've pursued Phase One in part I of this material. A significant outcome of that effort could be the discernment that it's time to transform an existing worship gathering or start a new one.
- Phase Two: *Form Launch Team.* To address worship head-on, you'll need a launch team.
- Phase Three: *Share Faith.* The launch team conducts outreach by entering the mission field to form connections, build trust, and share stories. The launch team expands with new members, not existing ones.
- Phase Four: *Ramp Up.* The launch team builds momentum beyond church walls through a variety of activities that introduce new people to what worship is and raise awareness of your specific project.
- Phase Five: *Launch Worship.* Launching is both a numerical and spiritual endeavor. You'll be ready for it if you have completed the work in the previous phases.

Parts II and III: Chapter organization:

- Completing steps for launching or relaunching worship, chapter by chapter, as laid out in the step-up charts.
- See the heading below, "Story Enhancements and Guides."

Part III: Inside and Outside Your Building

If you've ever studied film, you know the importance of the second act break, or "the point of no return." The concept is that the protagonist (main character) is forced to live with the decision they made about the conflict they went through, and can't go back. That describes you. Faith sharing and worship development are not one-and-done. Complete the step-up chart and your ongoing purpose to make new disciples in this segment.

References and Guides

The step-up charts

A key feature of this book, which helps you organize a process for worship development through faith sharing, is the step-up flowchart. You'll learn to use this tool as you go.

Jockeying around to absorb this material

This book encompasses a wealth of material and potentially new perspectives for participants. I've thought through places in the writing to help readers make connections between different parts of the book so that you can absorb it all over time. Use these symbols and directions at your discretion.

Play. Keep moving forward a step at a time.

Fast-forward. Jump ahead for planning purposes (implement later).

Rewind. Be sure you get this . . .

Pause. Reflect, rest, and pray before moving on.

Writing your own ending

Institutionalism may lead you to quit this work by convincing you that decline is inevitable. But institutionalism is a choice. So is faith. Decline is not inevitable if you take the journey seriously. You can rewrite your story to tell a new tale of hope and transformation to future generations. It's up to you.

Preface reflection questions

1. Say why and how what you just read was:
    - surprising,
    - engaging,
    - confusing,
    - encouraging, or
    - concerning.
2. Where did you see your church in what you read?
3. Where did you see yourself?
4. Who were you thinking about in what you just read?
5. What are you going to do next?

ACKNOWLEDGMENTS

Thanks to Scott Carlson, ICD (The Institute for Congregational Development), and the Wisconsin Annual Conference. You give me an annual platform that has allowed me to hone my teaching. You're an incredible support!

Ed Fenstermacher, I hope retirement is all you wanted. You were a great friend for many years. You have such a big heart for Jesus and the church. And you sent me so many clients and they taught me so much. You and they are in these pages.

Shout-out to my friend and former coach, Jim Griffith. You are a great friend to me and my family. And thanks for the encouragement to not clutch on the birdie putt. If I had more birdie putt ops, maybe I'd be able to reap the benefits of your teaching!

To all I've taught and coached to use this material as it was being produced, I give you a great big THANK YOU. You shaped the material as you used it. I have learned much from you.

Glenn Knepp, the in-depth conversations we had about transcendence and other heady topics were formative for what finally landed in print. I learned a lot about how to communicate what's in these pages while working with you.

Lori Wagner, I am grateful for your direct feedback on my material in the early stages. It helped me throw out the adiaphora and concentrate on what mattered.

The T, and the E. No words to express my love for you. You are my rock. Your support at such a time as this is a godly design. Your days will be long upon the land that the Lord thy God has given thee.

My little Lucy: I hope you pick this book up one day and see your name in it. Your name is written across my heart. I pray you can know the truths in this book. Some day.

My dear son Terry. I love you through eternity.

Husband Terry, you keep putting up with me through yet another new book. God has put us together, though it's not because I'm writing a book! Not many could put up with me the way you do in all aspects of our lives. You are my soulmate. And you're the best golfer I know personally. It's so fun to play with you.

Part I

INSIDE YOUR BUILDING

Chapter One

DISCERNING YOUR ROLE

Chapter Notes

Directors of plays give notes to the cast at the end of a performance so that actors can improve their next performance. The notes often focus on how the actor delivers a line or on a specific action they can take to add more meaning to a scene.

The chapter notes preface to each chapter serves a similar purpose in this material as the director's feedback in a play. Chapter notes provide direction to help you focus on the way you read the material so that you can make the most of the content.

Part I is laying groundwork. In chapter one of Part I, you lay the groundwork to lay the groundwork. The desired outcome for this chapter is for you to discern your role in developing an outward focus for worship in your church. But it might take you going through the entire workbook to determine how best to proceed, both personally and with your faith community. You won't have adequate insight into the demands you're facing until you pursue chapter one, and maybe even more. Keep an open mind and be ready to know that you don't know what you need to know—just yet.

Chapter Notes reflection question

What is your expectation of this chapter?

I. Real-Life Coaching Stories

Didn't work

Once upon a time, I had two different clients—one a worship leader and the other a solo pastor. Both leaders fell ill early in our coaching relationship and required significant time off to recover. I suggested we pause our coaching process, but both leaders wanted me to coach their people directly. I said yes; my bad. Both situations went south. Laypersons showed up to the coaching, confused and resistant. Who could blame them? Their leader had abandoned them, leaving them with a stranger. And it turned out that the older one was ready to retire. That created a dynamic of duplicity. The people I was coaching didn't blame their leader for the lack of progress. They blamed the coach. Of course, the coach should have never said yes to direct coaching of laypersons without their leader. It's common to coach laypersons alongside their leader, but not in place of. The leaders were AWOL, even if their illnesses provided them with an excuse to abandon ship.

Would've never worked

My client was enthusiastic about worship. But most members resented the modern changes he instituted to worship when he first arrived, before I started coaching him. The more changes he made, the more people he lost. Members stayed at the church but stopped serving. They dropped off boards and failed to show up for their traditional work commitments.

The leader had really wanted to start a new service, which is how I got connected with him. Two things were wrong about that focus. He kept saying the rural area had no new people. If that were true, then it would be hard to start a new service. Who would it be for? The members? They had already cast their vote. Additionally, there was excessive stress and dissension within the existing body because of the pastor. You can't start a new service during conflict and expect it to endure. Then something else happened that made the pastor mad. I knew he wouldn't stick it out.

Sorta worked

The pastor of the somewhat thriving church of about two hundred in worship was attempting to overhaul an existing service within just a few months. She had hired a worship leader whom she expected to take on the project. That's when I entered the scene as the coach. I suggested to the pastor that we apply the brakes and shift our focus to developing an outreach strategy, rather than an attractional one. She agreed. However, it quickly became clear to the worship leader that we were employing church planting strategies, which he wasn't prepared for. The worship leader declared he had no capacity for it. Therefore, the work of outreach fell to the pastor, and she was already too busy to build a new community between the church and the mission field—or at least she thought she was. We never really got to the point of training laypeople in faith sharing before the pastor decided it was time to return to the role of lead pastor. She mentioned in passing one day that one or two new families show up weekly to the service in question, so we did make some changes to it. The leader is satisfied with this increase. So be it.

Worked

One of my favorite clients ever came to me for worship development when he was appointed to a tiny rural church. He was scared to move in the direction we discussed. But he had a deep heart for people who knew Jesus, so he stepped up to the plate. They had a handful of members who wanted to do contemporary worship. I coached the pastor to pursue community connections rather than change style. They grew from about twenty in worship to about forty in about twenty-four months, before he got reappointed. The pastor then brought me along as his coach to his new appointment in a thriving area, at a larger church that had been languishing due to previous conflict and a lack of leadership. He turned things around with the same approach!

Working

My new client deeply loves his people and the place where he serves. That's an awesome place to begin any worship discussion. His church already has a presence in the community, but there has been no dedicated outreach. He is making connections to begin this process. He's a learner and isn't offended by the consideration of new ideas as expressed in these pages. His biggest learnings so far have been about himself. As a coach, you hope for clients that want to grow.

Coaching stories reflection questions

What points did the stories raise?

Did any describe you or your church? How?

II. Backstories of Institutionalism

Insights into the opening stories

The first story depicts leaders who didn't stick with their people to do what they were asking their people to do. The second story illustrates leadership's disregard for members even before outreach was introduced. Additionally, it reveals a misunderstanding of outreach. You can't reach out if there aren't people in your church's neighborhood, and if there is conflict in the existing body. The third story depicts a situation with significant potential and positive outcomes. However, because we moved too fast and settled for average results, outreach didn't pan out as well as it could have, and as planned. The last two stories depict leaders with a devotion to faith sharing and a willingness to follow a process for bringing others along.

The first worship service I ever started

In 1989, I was asked to head up the new "contemporary" worship service my church was planning to start. That was the word we used back then for what some now call "modern" worship. I had never started a service or led a band before. Additionally, I was not a serious Christian at the time. However, I had found my way to this traditional church, and the pastors knew I had a background in music and the arts. They nominated me for the lead position, and of course, I said yes; I'm a starter, although I didn't know it at the time. It sounded like fun!

The church had three services totaling about four hundred in worship. The pastors surveyed all members during all worship services on one Sunday. They asked whether members thought it was a good idea to go "contemporary" with worship in one of the services to attract newer, younger people. Overwhelmingly, members thought that was a good idea, if their service didn't change.

Oops. The pastors already knew it was going to be the 11 a.m. service that would change, as that's when they thought the young people would come. We started the new service three months later. That's fast. Too fast. Of the 125 that used to populate that service, only 40 attended the kickoff. It dropped even more after that. Members didn't participate in the other services as the pastors had expected. They went to different churches. Most never came back.

How institutionalism makes worship development dated in the twenty-first century

Today, I see leaders make the same assumptions we made in 1989. Most of my clients — including those in their twenties, thirties, and forties—are dated, and I do not refer to style. They move too quickly with worship changes, leaving members with whiplash. They blame members for their recalcitrance instead of understanding the dynamics of change. They think new people will show up. That's the most dated part of all.

And they minimize the likelihood of attrition among their members, as though members are robots who won't react. Underestimating the potential for conflict, especially in a smaller congregation, is a leadership deficit. It harms the process to go full steam ahead.

In my first startup experience, the result was, in fact, both harmful and successful. We grew back because there was still enough Christianity in the culture in 1989 for people to show up uninvited at church doorsteps. That has changed in the twenty-first century. Unthinking churches that cause harm in our modern-day secular culture don't recover, or at least not easily.

Plus, I wasn't really a serious follower of Christ back then. The non-churched culture is far too secular to put a marginal Christian in a lead position for worship. New people with whom you might make connections as the church want to meet Jesus, or they wouldn't be considering coming to your church. They're going to see through a worship leader who's not convinced that following Jesus is a life-changing, transformational choice.

Decades of decline and not talking about Jesus

Most churches in our modern church landscape have declined. Decline increases institutionalism: the overwhelming tendency to do things to save the church and take care of its members, resulting in the pursuit of quick and often poor decisions to check off a box.

The thing is that's not new. Church decline has been going on for decades. Yet church leaders are still blaming COVID-19 and many church splits over social issues for their decline. Real-life cultural dramas have indeed exacerbated the decline, but didn't cause it. For all the decline we've had for as long as we've had it, something else besides circumstances must be at work. I'll go out on a limb and say it's a lack of focus on Jesus, especially beyond church walls, but even behind them. When I have conducted consultations at declining churches, I've been hard-pressed to hear members discuss the power of Jesus in their own lives. Nor do I hear such expressions from the pulpit much. Christian churches revolve around Christ. To lose that centrality is to lose your identity. If a church doesn't revolve around Jesus internally, they won't externally either.

Case in point: During the COVID-19 pandemic, I experienced an influx of new clients who all wanted to know how to conduct online worship services *for their members*. They noticed that their online services were attracting a growing number of online drop-ins. They assumed that lurkers loved what they did, until they examined how many people logged on for less than a second. It's no wonder: You'd log on to a church service and see a picture of an empty sanctuary, and there would be slow, organ music playing in the background while awaiting someone to start things. How is that engaging? What if the church had done something to indicate Jesus is still in the building even if people weren't?

Case in point: During disaffiliations and church splits, churches were bogged down in voting and paying to separate from their tribes. Many churches lost a significant number of members, many members lost numerous friends, and all churches endured painful financial losses. They suffered greatly. But I never heard how a church struggling with the losses of disaffiliation still did the work of sharing Jesus beyond church walls, talking about how Jesus remains ever-present in the losses of life. Grief doesn't go away through talking about Jesus, but talking about Jesus during grief does allow you to share hope. The church is well versed in grief. Where was that expression between members and others they love in their own lives?

Culture change

Learning to talk about Jesus is a hurdle for mainliners. Our resistance to the *E* word (evangelism) is our fear that we're going to become evangelicals—standing on street corners espousing the four spiritual laws.

Learning to talk about Jesus isn't like that for a mainliner. It's more about faith sharing, not about convincing someone to "hear a gospel message and be saved." Our fears are our defensiveness. Defensiveness against being more overt about being a Christ follower is what we have to overcome.

Most church people want to be good disciples. But they don't connect discipleship with making new disciples. For many people, being a good disciple means living their life in a manner that honors God morally. Participating in public worship comes out of a sense of duty because it's what a good Christian disciple does. These are ingrained behaviors that you often see in churches with fewer than 250 in worship attendance. Learning to talk about Jesus comfortably and authentically is essential for helping members see discipleship as something more than just being a good person. That's culture change, and it's going to take time. Some experts say it takes up to seven years to change an organization's culture. That's part of why turning around your congregation is so hard. You must hang in there, even and especially when it doesn't seem like you're making progress.

Hanging in there is part of how faith takes root. You won't be without some encouragement, as you'll have inklings of fruit along the way. It won't all happen at once. And you'll have many hurdles to cross. You'll learn about those hurdles and how to get over them in this material. You can get over them. And your faith will grow as you do.

Putting the pieces in place to produce culture change

One way to move things along in your church will be to either transform existing worship or start a new service, or both. You won't start out pursuing this book study specifically to address in-person worship in your church. However, at some point, in a few weeks or months, if you continue to work through this material, you'll be faced with the decision to address in-person worship directly. You may lead this study and implement worship changes through a launch process a few times over a four- to seven-year time frame on your way to achieving enduring culture change in your church, from an inwardly focused to an outwardly focused approach.

And then you'll notice that you'll have nurtured about 20 percent of members and constituents who are seriously engaged in personal outreach in the community. Many of those participants will be new people. Wouldn't that be divine?

Backstories reflection questions

1. Say why and how what you just read was:
   - surprising,
   - engaging,
   - confusing,
   - encouraging, or
   - concerning.
2. Where did you see your church in what you read?
3. Where did you see yourself?
4. Who were you thinking about in what you just read?
5. What are you going to do next?

III. Rewriting the Story of Your Church's Future

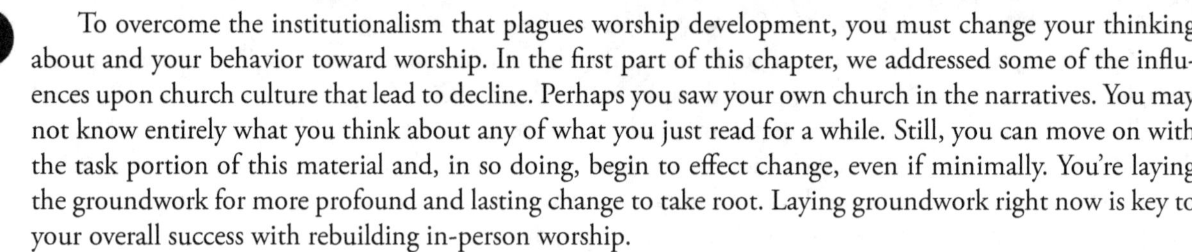

To overcome the institutionalism that plagues worship development, you must change your thinking about and your behavior toward worship. In the first part of this chapter, we addressed some of the influences upon church culture that lead to decline. Perhaps you saw your own church in the narratives. You may not know entirely what you think about any of what you just read for a while. Still, you can move on with the task portion of this material and, in so doing, begin to effect change, even if minimally. You're laying the groundwork for more profound and lasting change to take root. Laying groundwork right now is key to your overall success with rebuilding in-person worship.

Some regrouping before taking on the to-dos in this chapter could be to:

- review the outline for going through this material in the preface under the heading Developing Your Story's Plotline,

- pray that God will give you discernment as you move through the next part of this chapter,

- get familiar with and communicate the outreach process that's different from what members might expect:
    - o Ask a friend out for coffee, go for a walk with them, or do something else.
    - o Pray before you go that God would open the door to faith talk.
    - o Have a conversation in which you're listening to your friend.
    - o Allow God to tap you on the shoulder when it's time to say something profound or applicable about your own faith journey.
    - o Ask if it's okay to share but don't do it if they say no, and don't be offended either. They'll probably say yes though.
    - o See what they say.
    - o Set a time to be together again.

Remember: The central behavior that enables you to recognize God's prompting to share faith in any conversation is prayer. You will not learn how to share your faith without beseeching God to help you learn to share it, and then actually share it.

Consider this plan for implementing the to-dos for this chapter:

- Look over the step-up chart to the right.
- Read the entries associated with the to-do list.
- Make your plan for completing the tasks.
- Implement your plan according to your timeline.

Discerning Your Role

1. Increase spiritual practices
2. Expect resistance (to item 1)
3. Discern your role
4. Address your schedule
5. Establish a timeline
6. Go public
7. Gather participants
8. Start or transform worship
9. Prepare to talk/ count cost
10. See fruit

One to four weeks

A column like this appears in every chapter to outline your to-dos for pursuing the material in that chapter. The suggested timeline at the bottom outlines the typical timeframe required for most churches to complete the actions. You can extend the recommended timeline in each column in part I, but not in part II. In this chapter, you'll consider how to take your initial participants in this study through this part of the material (part I). Prepare to amend the timeline.

1. Increase spiritual practices

The single most important thing you can do to become a faith sharer is to pray to become one. Prayer focuses you and allows you to surrender to God's power. If you go out shopping and pray before you go that God will open the doorway to faith conversations with someone, you've put God in charge. And you've focused your shopping trip to be ready for God to show up.

Prayer and other spiritual practices are disciplines. Christianity is a disciplined approach to life. Lots of church leaders will say that they talk to God all day, or they pray when they're on the treadmill, for example. There's nothing wrong with either of those actions. But are you still praying even if you don't get your workout in that day? What if you had such a busy day that you never got in one word with God, but thought you did because you did it the day before? Without a dedicated and systematic approach to prayer, it's easy to disconnect.

In your own way and style:

- calendar your prayer life to include regular, repeated contact with God;
- add in fasting, silence, and other disciplines;
- ask God to prepare you for the mission field, where you can share your faith; and
- ask God to prepare the mission field.

What is your plan to increase spiritual practices in your life? Write it down and calendar your start date!

2. Expect resistance (to item #1)

Increasing your prayer practices grows you. You notice the fruit of the Spirit in yourself. You might like the changes in yourself, or not—the same with others in your life toward you. You're changing, so you're behaving differently. That's threatening to people around you.

Prayer is both a means of support for outreach efforts and simultaneously part of the conflict associated with outreach. It's a deep irony. Humans want predictability in life. Prayer reveals that we don't really have it. Those dynamics will cause you to resist the discipline associated with personal spiritual growth and corporate worship development if you're a church leader. You'll doubt that a disciplined prayer approach is any different from a random one. It is. However, you must develop discipline to recognize that.

Examine your heart to see if you have any resistance to beginning a more disciplined approach to prayer. Write your confession to God and ask for the courage to change your habits!

3. Discern your role (calling)

This workbook is broken into three parts. Part I is a study of worship and the connection to outreach. Your first discernment task is to see if you're going to take on part I, and if so, who is going to lead it.

If your church has fewer than one hundred in worship, the lead pastor/solo pastor is likely to lead the study with their people. If your church has over one hundred participants in prayer, you can likely find someone in the body to lead it, whether a layperson or a paid staff member.

Regardless of your size or organizational approach to using this material, the lead pastor must do the work of faith sharing beyond the church walls if you want others in your church to do it. The lead or solo pastor doesn't have to personally handle every task listed in part I. You can hand off some to others if you see to it that they get completed. But unless you pursue personal faith sharing beyond the church walls, it won't matter what else you do. Worship changes won't stick. Additional caveats to pursuing part I include:

- Preview the material. If the lead pastor is going to hand off leadership of the study to someone else, it is recommended that the lead pastor know what's coming. Take a gander through the entire book and do some of the exercises along the way.
- Set aside time. Part I requires approximately three to five hours per week to develop for your people and lead the study.
- Streamline your schedule. See the next heading.

What are your initial thoughts about how your congregation can best use this book and your specific role in using it?

4. Address your schedule

Leaders of churches with over one hundred in worship have usually had to address their schedule by eliminating things that don't matter much in their church's specific context. Those things don't involve many people, or someone else can lead them in your place.

Leaders of churches with fewer than one hundred in worship struggle to let things go. The institutional church would have you work sixty-five hours a week to be available to the members. It's okay to take on new projects as long as you don't give up the old. You'll have to resist the dynamic to be everything to your people if you want to impact in-person worship, and more important, if you're going to grow as a leader or even just as a person who follows Jesus.

Making time to share your faith and bring others along with you to do the same is the pinnacle of being a Christ follower. I spend a lot of time in coaching addressing schedules to help leaders live into their potential. So we're going to spend some time streamlining now!

How to streamline your existing work schedule for a leader: Free up (don't add) three to five hours per week on an existing schedule to lead part I. To make this process stick, do the following:

- Make a list of the things you do that drain you.
- Hand off leadership to someone you've mentored.
- Let things go that involve so few people that hardly anyone would notice the change.
- Plan to help volunteers hand off some of their existing commitments to your church to be part of this study by following the same process as you.

Read the stories of three clients who are pursuing schedule changes below in order to provide context for what are often new behaviors.

The pastor of three small churches wanted to know how to focus on one of the three congregations more than the others with rebuilding in-person worship. She told me about a retired pastor who is part of one of the congregations. She has already given him some visibility in leadership. Members like him. She hadn't tied that to handing off things like pastoral care and even preaching in two of the three churches. We discussed a more formal approach to do that, which would free up some of her time for the one church.

The pastor of the busy church in the opening coaching story, "Working," is taking the streamlining of his schedule seriously. He's talking about grief. He recognizes that he is going to have to give up some of the schmoozing he likes to do with parishioners and new people in order to be more organized as he's gathering new people. That's how this should feel: new and somewhat demanding. The good news is that the thing that he's good at—talking with people—isn't going to change, and he will reshape that gift as he progresses with cutting back. God has made us who we are. Those gifts don't go away!

Most pastors of churches with fewer than 250 worshipers struggle to determine who to include in studying and implementing *Rebuilding In-Person Worship*. They automatically want to include the people who are already doing everything. Perhaps those are the ones to select, but asking them to add more to an existing schedule isn't fair to the volunteer. Part of the coaching process is to help the leader guide the volunteer in thinking through how they can hand off three to five hours of their work to someone else.

This is the time to do one thing you just read about. See how it goes, then do another. By the time you get to part 2 in this workbook, you should have made significant progress in cutting back. Keep praying!

What will you do first?

5. Establish a timeline

The leader of this initial study (part I) lays the groundwork for your congregation to pursue worship development through faith sharing. You can't do part II without part I. You can determine how to pursue part I to suit your style and size. Consider these options:

- Scenario one: Do the study in six to eight weeks, along with some of the tasks. Make plans to complete the tasks you didn't get to over the next few months.
    - Upside: exposing book-study participants to the big picture of worship development
    - Possible downside: minimizing tasks to get them done quickly
- Scenario two: Study one chapter a month in part I to complete ongoing tasks as you go.
    - Upside: getting a deeper understanding of the chapter
    - Possible downside: losing sight of the big picture of worship development
- Scenario three: something you create
    - Upside: contextual and local; that carries
    - Possible downside: not doing all the tasks because you have your own ideas.
- Scenario four: Skip ahead to chapter 4 to consider the approach laid out underneath the Step-Up column. Larger churches may like this option.

- Scenario five: Provide workbooks for a select group of members to go through on their own, while you go through it on your own as the leader.
    - Upside: takes less time for the leader
    - Possible downside: not scheduling time for interaction or completing tasks

What approach do you like? Calendar your intentions!

6. Go public (with messaging: for leaders and lay participants in this study)

Church leaders influence members through various forms of messaging. Use that dynamic to encourage members to engage in outreach. It happens this way:

- Leaders go out into the neighborhood beyond the church to share their faith. They return to the faith community to share the experience within the existing faith community.
- Leaders are not just the pastors leading the process forward. Leaders are participants too. We all have circles of influence in which we can share what God is doing to change us.

Ways to get out into the neighborhood include local opportunities, such as:

- Spending time in a coffee shop. That's where you got to know the barista who liked you until they realized you were from the church. When you asked them to sit down over a cup of their famous brew, they declined. It stung, but you're still standing, despite the rejection. That's a story to tell. If you're a preacher, that story will fit with a sermon about self-esteem, forgiveness, building trust, and making assumptions about people. It will also fit into a conversation over coffee with your friend from church.

  - Are you praying for your person now? Were you before?

- Having HH (Happy Hour) at the VFW. That's when you struck up a conversation with someone who, when they realized you're from the church, started "asking for a friend" about what your church thought about LGBTQ+. Turns out the friend was his daughter. You had prayed before you went into the bar for a conversation like this to take place. Tell that story!

- If you tell your story in a sermon or in a personal conversation, you can highlight how you were able to espouse church values to bless your person, and how you prayed before you went in. That will be encouraging to members and others in your circles of influence.

- This week, pursue a faith conversation with someone you know who isn't in your church. Find a way to connect it to your messaging.

7. Gather participants

Rule one: Don't ask people to "help me with worship development" when gathering people to participate in this study. They'll say no. They will only view this as too much time commitment because you weren't clear. Or, if they say yes, they will be doing it to help you, not to grow in their own faith personally. And then they'll come to resent their yes and resent you too.

Rule two: Develop a process of recruiting that's clear and missionally focused:

- Pray. Ask God to guide your process. Ask God who to include in the study.
- Make a list. Write down names that come to mind through prayer.
- Add or subtract. With whom do you want to work? If you don't feel a sense of compatibility with someone on your list, cross out their name for now.
- Reach out to each person on your list individually.

- Say, "God has put you on my heart. I'm wondering where you feel you are on your spiritual journey and whether you're interested in taking another step toward growth."
- Describe the study, the timeline, the time commitment, the material, and the desired outcome. Tell them that you're only asking them to be involved in this study. There is a part II to this work. They can agree to participate in that or not. You're not asking them to do that now. You're just asking for part I—no strings attached.
- If they agree, provide the book and your own insight about the material.
- Make a first reading assignment (volume 1, preface and chapter 1).
- Spend some time in prayer to create an initial list of individuals to include in this study. Please write down your process for reaching out to them and calendar it.

8. Start or transform worship

If you get through part I of this book, then you're at a turning point in the action. You can either start a new service, transform existing worship, or both, or neither. It could be months before you know which. That means praying and discerning between now and then. Consider some factors.

If your church is over one hundred in worship and you want to start a new service:

You can start something entirely new or duplicate what you already have. Either way, the process will be the same. You'll pursue outreach through church planting as the primary way to gather new people. If you duplicate what you already have in worship, you'll be tempted not to pursue part II of this material. That will be a mistake because you'll be relying on members to populate the pews or folding chairs, and also attraction to grow the service. Many churches make the mistake of asking their members to come to the new service. The members don't want to. That's how the service declines before it ever gets going.

If your church is under one hundred in worship and you want to start a new service:

If your space is small and you're filling it up, you can still duplicate what you already have if your existing service is at critical mass for your area.

You can read ahead to chapter 5 to learn about the concept of critical mass. Caveat: Pursue part II to achieve your goal of starting your new service even if you're duplicating it.

Another caveat: Before deciding to duplicate what you already do, read chapter 2 and consider the impact of quality on worship development.

Transforming existing worship first

If your church is tiny (under thirty in worship), consider transforming the existing worship service first if you aren't at critical mass for that service. You might need to consider pursuing multiple launch processes to reach your minimum number. That's doable, but only under certain conditions. You'll learn about that in part II, phase 4, entry 36. Consider not reading ahead as it might be TMI (Too Much Information). But, that's up to you.

Transforming existing worship while you're starting a new service

If you're under or over one hundred in worship and have reached critical mass in the existing worship service, and you want to start a new service, you can still relaunch the existing service to grow around faith sharing. It can be more doable than you might think to do two at once. All of part II lays out the process of developing your people. You can train and encourage different groups simultaneously. Each group that you train will have the focus of their faith community, or worship service that they attend. That's not a recommendation. It's just something to consider, depending on your capacity.

Stopping altogether

Sometimes, the only possible leader for this study in your church is the lead pastor. And they don't have the bandwidth to take on this process as outlined in this chapter at this time. It's appropriate to hit the pause button. But do so with self-reflection. Many leaders are personally scared of outreach and of their people. Don't let those dynamics be the thing that stops you.

Asking people to work through the book on their own

You can provide copies of this material for your members to review on their own while you regroup as a leader. See entry #5 in this chapter.

Spend some time flipping through the charts and teaching entries in part II to see what you'll be doing should you decide to pursue transforming existing worship or starting a new service. What conclusions did you draw?

9. Prepare to talk with your board (Count the cost)

If you get to the end of part I and decide you want to pursue worship in more overt ways, it's time to have a conversation with your board. Count the cost with them.

- Money. There is little financial cost associated with part I of *Rebuilding In-Person Worship.* If you're starting a new service, the potential financial outlay goes up significantly. You may hire a point person, find a new venue, hire a worship leader, increase technology, and retain a coach.[1]
- Time. The startup timeline is nine to eighteen months, although closer to two years with your work in part I. That timeline will impact your church and leadership.
- Conflict. The worship startup process may cause conflict and resistance. Scratch that. *Will.*
- Transformation. Pursuing faith sharing beyond church walls leads to both numerical and spiritual growth. Adding new people will change the church's needs.
- Inaction. What happens to your church if you don't take on the challenges associated with faith sharing and worship development?

Calendar when you think you should speak with your board about this material.

10. See fruit

As you move along through part I and then into part II, you may struggle to see progress. But it's there. Find it, lift it, and encourage the body with it. It may include:

- developing faith-sharing videos to play in worship;
- engaging people from the mission field in sermon development;

- receiving a spontaneous endorsement for your pursuit of mission from an unlikely source;
- experiencing a failed attempt at an outreach activity by the church, with the participants seeing that they missed some steps in this material; or
- getting wind of a supportive comment for your church leadership that one member made to another when the other member was derogatory at a church event.

Pray now that God will allow you to see fruit in your efforts to share faith for rebuilding in-person worship. Make a list of the fruit you hope to see and when you hope to see it.

Rewriting your story reflection questions:

1. Say why and how what you just read was:
   - surprising,
   - engaging,
   - confusing,
   - encouraging, or
   - concerning.
2. Where did you see your church in what you read?
3. Where did you see yourself?
4. Who were you thinking about in what you just read?
5. Additional chapter questions:
   - What's the role of prayer in pursuing this study?
   - Do you think you'll lead this study or find someone else to do it? Why?
   - What timeline are you considering for pursuing this study?
   - Who are you thinking of to include in pursuing it with you? When will you reach out to them?

What are you going to do next? 

Chapter Postscript: Some People Know Things

I've considered making myself a t-shirt: I *golf* and I *know* things. I love the game of golf. Plus, I know things.

Perhaps you've heard of the late, great Lyle Schaller, although if you're under fifty or maybe even sixty, you probably haven't. He was a brilliant church strategist who wrote many books about church dynamics and growth. I had an opportunity to spend some time with him when I was starting a new church. He was witty. He gave me some insight into myself. He told me (about me), "Some people know things." That would be me. Discernment is my number one spiritual gift, if you care about that sort of thing. You must recognize that:

- I've never been a senior or a solo pastor. But I learned *a ton* about the role when I was director of church planting at a megachurch.
- I learned about church structure in the megachurch, where you'll find departmental leaders. Few, if any, of them could have ever led an entire church that size, as they were primarily small-venue leaders pastoring "congregations" of about one hundred or fewer.

All those experiences, along with my specific wiring, allow me to impart that knowledge to you. That said, I'm not you. You'll need to trust what I know enough to apply it to your context, where you are the expert. And then trust yourself enough to know how to keep what's going to work and discard what isn't. Your personal discernment and confession will allow you to understand your motivations.

Chapter Two

LEADING WORSHIP

Chapter Notes

This chapter is about the nature of worship. It's designed to go deep. That makes it demanding. You may not agree with all the ideas presented. Your disagreement with me could be the launchpad for your own identity in worship. So could your agreement. Either way, own your ideas to share them. Read this chapter somewhat analytically.

Chapter Notes reflection question

What is your expectation of this chapter?

I. Real-Life Coaching Stories

Fun Church

The church had been in the throes of a significant struggle, during which many people left. A friend of mine was a member. She called the church "fun church." The day she took me as her guest, I knew why. The message . . . wow. The preacher confessed his own duplicity in the drama the church had come through. He identified mistakes staff made, without naming names or implicating individuals. He spoke about not living in a community. He talked about members' failure to think about people outside the church, in favor of an inward focus. I've shared that message with many leaders as I've coached them. Several have been horrified by this pastor's public display of authenticity. Maybe that's because you're told in preaching classes not to "vomit" all over people with your own needs. Fair enough. But this pastor wasn't acting needy. He was acting pastoral and missional, which included some come-to-Jesus moments. The pastor had a backbone. The music was fun. That's what fun church meant to my friend. It was fun because the environment was real. Otherwise, it would have been a show.

Big Church

Would that I had a nickel for every time I heard a church say "We don't wanna be a megachurch." I often respond, "I don't think you're in any danger of becoming one." People usually laugh. But I'm serious. My response is a critique couched in humor. Smaller churches think megachurches are all about entertainment. I was on staff at a megachurch, and I knew the worship leaders personally. One of them was an incredible musician and one of the most natural, authentic, and faithful worship leaders I've ever known. It was common to see people in seats weeping during the praise set.

Some would make their way to the prayer chapel because of it. Or they'd contact you the next day because they wanted to deepen their faith. The reason I respond somewhat teasingly and sarcastically to members who say they don't want to be megachurches is that most churches haven't recognized their own institutionalism when they say something like that. A church's institutionalism is going to stop you from growth if you don't address it. Growth is not about you. It's about extending your church's footprint to connect new people to Jesus and the church. All Christians are called to that belief and behavior. It's not like megachurches aren't institutional. But they don't typically do things to keep their doors open or make decisions to satisfy members like smaller churches do. They got over that tendency a long time ago. Most megachurches focus on new people and train members to do outreach. Plus, very few leaders are wired with the God-given capability to grow a church that large. So don't worry. Your church isn't going to increase to that size. But it can grow healthier and thus engage more people within a framework that your pastor can lead. Megachurches can do things smaller churches can't, and vice versa. Your church doesn't need to be a megachurch to learn from them, or to be missional and practical.

Mainline Church

I got to know the pastor of a mid-sized mainline church during COVID. He attended an online training I did and had me work with his church on a few worship areas. The pastor was personally engaged in outreach before I ever connected with him. He had incredible stories about people from the community who didn't attend his church but began to think of him as their pastor and his church as their church. They had a blended, in-person gathering led primarily by volunteers. The worship leader was not at the level of a musician in my megachurch. But he was fun, engaging, and good enough. Their worship setting was small. They could seat about fifty in one room at one time. They had three services at that size. It was a positive environment. Would you see people weeping there? I think it could happen, although in such a small setting, a person who was crying would be more exposed. Not a megachurch. Still effective.

Coaching stories reflection questions

- What points did the opening stories raise?
- Did any story describe you or your church? How?

II. Backstories of Institutionalism

Insights into the opening stories

The three stories you just read depict engaging worship. If the services weren't engaging, members wouldn't be inviting their friends. Members and other regulars must be involved and engaged in their own public worship gatherings for new people to connect.

That new people won't engage if members don't is a dynamic rooted in the value of community. What's community? It was described (though not defined) in all three opening stories, though each community is unique.

If you reread the stories, look for the value of community behind the scenes. Compare your insights to the following.

What's community, and how might it develop?

Community is a sense of belonging. People share, even if they don't know one another well. A community needs values to create a sense of belonging.

Outreach is a value that creates community. Sharing a value of outreach doesn't mean every member will be gung-ho about sharing faith beyond church walls. But burgeoning disciples reticent to share their faith to make new disciples may still grasp that outreach is the primary identity of that specific community. Even if they don't do it personally, it's meaningful to be part of an organization that espouses that value. The value of the community as a faith-sharing community beyond church walls will influence them over time, unless or until it doesn't. That burgeoning disciple might not stick around if the value of faith sharing doesn't engage them. Those who do esteem that value are in a different place.

It's like when I went to Target Field to see a concert of one of my now-favorite entertainers (who wasn't exactly on my radar as a top pick to pay money to see before I went to the concert).

Part of something

In August 2023, my husband and I went to see a colorful singer with our Orlando friends. It was their idea. We went to be with our friends. We took the light rail (public transportation). The further we got into the city, the more different we were from those getting on the train after us; we so suburban, they so urban. Still, all of us fans had a lot to talk about on the train, to and from the concert, despite our different looks and styles. A value connected us: attending a concert to see someone we all liked or going with people we liked. We didn't even talk about the superstar we were going to see with those who got on the train after us. We just interacted and connected because we were headed to the same place. It was fun.

During the concert, I turned to my friend and said, "Wow, this is like worship." My friend and her husband are both pastors. My husband isn't. Lucky him, says he. But he thought the concert was worship-like too.

The athletic, acrobatic, musical, creative blonde singer was our worship leader, so to speak. She had a lot to say about many things, whether she spoke or sang them. However, it was the camaraderie of people influenced by the same dynamics in the same space that had the most significant impact on my experience. When I looked around the massive outdoor space and saw 45,000 of my closest friends packed into Target Field to see my new favorite singer, they were all doing the same thing I was: hanging out to the music and jamming. Well, not all of them were. It was a massive crowd after all. But so many of them were! The colorful singer who matched the color I wore to celebrate the concert sold me on her talent and heart. Maybe she also did that with many of the others who came to the concert to hang out with their friends. For sure, many of that crowd came to see her because they really wanted to even if they had to drag their friends along. Talk about feeling connected.

What's worship?

- Worship is a gathering of disciples of various levels of belief who gather as a community to publicly express their love of God to the degree that they want to express themselves, according to their beliefs.
- Overt, public expression grows when the worship gathering is engaging rather than distracting and when there is a central purpose that regular attendees value.
- Regulars influence new people, because new people won't engage if regulars don't.
- A concert is not worship, but we can still learn from it.

The quality of the worship experience as learned from a concert

- If in a concert venue that sat 45,000 people, there was no Jumbotron on which you could watch the performer, you would barely be engaged because, from a distance, the performer looks like an ant.
- The growing size of the crowd and the room that accommodates it requires more and better technology.
- Additionally, the musical quality of a concert that you attend is part of what draws you in. You would expect nothing less than perfection.

The lack of quality for churches under 250 in worship

Churches don't need to be perfect artistically for disciples to be engaged, although megachurches come close to perfection. But that's because of their size. Before they were mega, they likely strove to be very good. Their quality improved as they added more people, because they had to address issues such as size, space, content, and relevance to accommodate an increasing number of users. They also likely had a central purpose: to make new disciples. Megachurches are typically very concerned with sharing the gospel with people.

Smaller churches must also address quality, but only to the degree necessary to be good enough for their current size. Smaller churches often struggle to understand the concept of size or the value of being "good enough."

Tiny churches commonly meet in spaces that are far too large for the group. The space dwarfs the experience because there aren't enough people in it for them to connect, let alone connect with the worship experience. There may not be enough tech for the room they're in. However, ironically, it's more common that the tech is adequate for the room's size but not necessary for the group's size, since the group doesn't fill the room. The way the tech is run is inadequate for the technology. Tech and the size of the community are out of step with each other and with the technology itself. That's harmful to the worship experience because it impedes the engagement of the disciples who gather.

A worship quality checklist

Worship quality is best measured not by style but by:

- making the room fit the size of the group,
- making sure technology doesn't glitch,
- producing singable music,
- putting together a good worship flow,
- developing sermons that are relevant to the lives of members and the people they care about, and
- getting input on messages from members and the people they care about.

That's the list that makes you good enough. If you can check off that entire list, then you have a decent quality of service. The questions to ask are, Is good enough good enough for you? Should it be? How can you make your service great? Do you want it to be great? You can make your service great by focusing on the primary value that draws the community together: sharing faith beyond church walls. The power of your missional focus will bring life to your public gathering. Good quality worship is just a performance without a missional focus. A church that focuses on performance is exclusive: for members only. It's superficial, and that's not what new people are looking for in a church.

The result of tepid, poor-quality worship: exclusivity and toxicity

Tepid and otherwise poor-quality worship (according to the above list under the previous bullet) is exclusive. It's for members only because new people won't want to be part of it. New people want substance. They want to be moved. If you, the church regular or member, are not moved by the worship gathering, then new people won't be. They'll see your lack of expression and chalk it up to a lack of connection with God.

A members-only church doesn't fit the definition of a church of disciples gathering to worship before God. Disciples care about new people coming to know Jesus. A members-only church is plagued by toxicity that cares only about the members. The toxic church grows homogeneous because no one who wants to be a disciple of Jesus can learn how to be one in that church.

Put yourself in the place of a new person. If someone seeking faith has the option to choose between an overtly expressive church and an ingrown, members-only church, which do you think they'd choose?

The invisible church

If church members don't value an outwardly focused church life, it's tough to do ministry in your location. Your church is invisible. No one knows you exist. You're a members-only group. Stories abound about how churches that want to change start by doing community interviews only to find that no one in the neighborhood knows they're there, yet they drive by the building every day. Truth.

When your value as a faith community is to tell others about Jesus, new people will form a relationship with your church through you. Or someone who has connected with your church through you or someone else in your church will tell others in their circle of influence about the good work your church is doing.

A church must be concerned about its reputation. Members-only churches don't even have a reputation. Compare that to a megachurch. Which church do you think does more ministry?

The impact of worship leading on developing community and visibility

The lack of members' engagement during public worship is another way to describe institutionalism. One way for churches to reverse the institutional nature of worship is for members to think of themselves as worship leaders. That's the central theme of this chapter: Everyone in your church is a worship leader by virtue of their worship. Therefore, they have a responsibility to produce the worship gathering, which they do with their worship. Their engagement increases when they see themselves as worship leaders, because worship leaders make new disciples beyond the church walls.

Most churches with fewer than 250 worshipers have had sufficient exposure in our present day to larger, influential churches, from which they draw inspiration for worship leading. The term "worship leader" is a standard reference for up-front leaders, specifically lead musicians and song leaders. Your church can go one better. You can help members see themselves as worship leaders in ways that may even surpass those of larger churches. Most church leaders do not communicate that members and other worship regulars at the worship gathering are worship leaders *by virtue of their own worship*. It's as though leaders and members accept the decline and take no action to fight back. Rethinking and identifying worship leading roles is part of fighting back.

How to encourage members as worship leaders and create a reputation

When members see themselves as worship leaders, it builds community. Members won't see themselves that way unless their leaders do and thus communicate to the members what they see. For example, during the worship gathering, someone can say, "I'm so grateful for your worship," or "I'm so thankful to see the Holy Spirit in action," or "You are leading me in prayer today."

You can also write about what a worship leader is in church communications. You can speak about it at meetings. You can post about it on social media. You don't need to say much. You need to say a few things regularly and repeatedly. The more members see themselves as worship leaders, the more outwardly focused they grow.

BYOJ engagement

A profoundly impactful reality of naming Holy Spirit activity in the gathered community is the power of joy, which lifts the community of faith and literally builds it. Worship participants who pursue faith development beyond the church walls with new people are themselves being changed. They begin to recognize their role as worship leaders. They become concerned about their ability to express their gratitude to God during the public gathering.

They Bring Your Own Joy (BYOJ) to the public gathering because they are experiencing personal transformation as they see themselves anew: I'm a disciple who makes disciples! They hear themselves in their own voice sharing faith beyond church walls, and it's a game-changer. Being a disciple who makes disciples is the pinnacle of being a faithful follower of Christ. It's joyful!

Claiming joy doesn't mean you're not going to be sad sometimes. It doesn't imply that you can't go to the worship service with some regrets. Joy implies vulnerability. It's a fruit of the Spirit! We are all vulnerable before God. Life is filled with loss. Joy allows us to sorrow before God. When some in the gathered community can't connect with their own joy that day, it's others' joy that covers their sorrow. And somehow that allows the grieving person the encouragement to step out of their grief for a season of healing. That's the nature of community. Remember that, worship leader.

Subjective authenticity

When you see joy in a public worship gathering, it's because members brought it with them. No one can manufacture that joy, not even great musicians who lead worship from the front. Not even people in seats who are rapt in prayer can make it up. You can tell just by looking and watching a person in the seats or an up-front leader whether that person is overtly expressing themself in the public gathering to draw attention to themselves instead of really being there to meet God. Or can you?

In story one at the beginning of this chapter, did you consider the preaching pastor to be authentic, like I did? You weren't there, but perhaps you can sense the vibe just from reading the story. If you have ever worshiped at a megachurch, did you notice people weeping, as depicted in story two? Did their weeping completely turn you off? Did you consider that the person weeping might be having an awful day? Were you having a bad day that day and therefore couldn't absorb someone else's emotion? Maybe the worship leader was having a bad day and said or did something offhand that put a stumbling block in front of you, and you didn't like the tone in her voice. It sounded . . . manipulative. Those are all reasons why you might think what is happening in a megachurch or any other public worship gathering is inauthentic, when the friend who brought you happens to love it.

And just as any person in the seats can perceive an up-front leader as engaging or overbearing, people in seats perceive one another in those ways. New people connect to the worship experience, or not, even before the music begins. No matter how authentic disciple-making disciples are in the public gathering, either before, during, or after it, some people aren't going to like you. But no one will like you if you're not in a public gathering simply because you're so grateful and want to share your gratitude.

Transcendent: The central dynamic that influences worship development

The member can and does influence the guest during the public worship gathering with their authentic worship. Except it's God who is the influencer.

We stated in the preface that God is present in public worship in ways that are not visible elsewhere in church life. That's why we should honor public gatherings by rebuilding them. *Re*build, don't just start to build from where you are, as you're not in a position of strength. Part of rebuilding is learning to see God's activity in the gathered community. No one can fully articulate God's behavior in a way that honors God, since God is God and we are not. That's why our relationship with God is worship. We can only attempt to grasp some godly dynamics so that we can honor God in how we come together publicly.

Public worship is God's deal. God cares if we show up. We show up to it more than bodily when we pursue faith beyond church walls. God can and does, then, use our transformation and engagement to influence others. That's what honoring God in the public gathering looks like.

A church welcomes a guest by creating a powerful worship experience that believers in Jesus (even if they're not members) can engage with. Theoretically, your members are believers in Jesus. You might have regulars who aren't members, and some new people could already be Christ followers. Worship is a gathering of disciples of different levels of belief. The expressive worship of a believer can help a less devoted disciple become more dedicated when it is authentic. God can use our worship to impact someone else.

In any public worship gathering, God is the sum of the parts, because we gather for a singular purpose: to praise God. But God is also greater than the sum of the parts, because of what God does in the public gathering. God can use the worship of a person in a seat or in front of the congregation to influence someone struggling with faith toward faith. That's God's transcendence, and it's a paradox. Only God can use our worship to influence others when it is genuine and authentic, and exists solely to praise God, not to influence anyone. You and I do not go to "perform worship" to influence our guests, even though we invited them there.

We go to worship to be us. Worship leading, community building, and making new disciples are what make "you do you" as a Christ follower. God will influence the guest through you when you are you. God doesn't have to do that either. Christ followers have zero input over the guest's connection. We can prepare for it, but we cannot control it. How freeing is *that*?

Designed for believers but with the guest in mind

- Performing hits: that's what the featured entertainer does in a concert. Worship hits include old hymns done to encourage participation.
- Doing covers: sometimes the featured entertainer performs someone else's hit, but in their own style. Doing covers includes updating the style of a hymn or traditionalizing the style of a modern praise song.
- Not asking you what kind of music you like. No one ever reached out to me from the concert I attended to see who my favorite entertainer is, so they could do their songs (it's Steven Tyler, btw).
- Performing for existing fans and engaging the fans' friends in the process. Gearing worship to the believers so that they'll participate. That doesn't mean ignoring the singability of songs and not fixing glitchy technology. You still must put together a quality worship experience.

The true diversity that comes through faith sharing beyond church walls

The level of diversity I observed at the concert I attended in August 2023 was truly remarkable. I saw it on the train on the way there, and every time I left my seat to do something else in the stadium. It's true at concerts, and it's true in the church: diversity comes through authenticity.

Most mainline churches are concerned with diversity and inclusivity. The question is, How does that occur? It occurs when you begin inviting people you've been discipling to your church. That's when you have the potential to grow more diverse. You will reach out to people you know who are in your circle of influence. But they're not exactly like you. Then that person learns how to reach out to people in their circle of influence whom they know and like, but who aren't exactly like them. The new person that the person you invited has now invited is also at least once removed from you. So they might be even less like you than the person you invited who invited them. That's what making disciples does for a church: it creates diversity.

Look around your church right now. You're not a church that is making new disciples, and you're homogeneous. I see it every time I conduct a site visit in a church that claims to value diversity.

Time to start something new

You have a lot of capacity within an existing worship service to introduce new elements that keep you culturally relevant without alienating or rebuffing your regular attendees. You can design worship with well-executed music that your regular attendees will relate to and use technology to convey your message effectively without overdoing it for the size of your room. And yet you can still do some new things that a new person will relate to, even if the member doesn't, without really changing the style of your worship. You might call that worship blended. I'm not opposed to blended worship, unlike some church growth experts. All worship is combined if you're continuing to try new things, so that you can add meaning to the experience within the framework of that experience.

But while you have a lot of capacity to make changes to existing worship without throwing the baby out with the bathwater, you don't have eternal capacity. At some point and through the invitational process of making new disciples, you're going to have reached the limit of diversity that describes that one gathering. You might find you want to reach out to a group of people who live in the area right outside your church, but won't participate in the existing service because they don't culturally fit in. Few who participate in that service know anything about that population. It's not the music or the service's style that's the problem. It's that very few in your church have connections with that demographic.

Now it's time to start something new that represents a very different style and target. Follow the same process of making new disciples, and you'll bear fruit.

Backstories reflection questions

1. Say why and how what you just read was:
    - surprising,
    - engaging,
    - confusing,
    - encouraging, or
    - concerning.
2. Where did you see your church in what you read?
3. Where did you see yourself?
4. Who were you thinking about in what you just read?
5. What are you going to do next?

III. Rewriting Your Church's Story

Leading Worship

IMPLEMENT

11. Worship leader dynamics
12. Space dynamics
13. Flow dynamics
14. Confessional (interactive) prayer
15. Sermon prep community

One to many weeks

Your ability as a faith community to add and subtract worship elements in your environment to make worship meaningful to members and regulars, so that they can invite their guests, will grow from your interaction with everything you've read so far. There's not one right way to put a worship service together. There are only better ways to help members engage and, in turn, include their friends.

In this section, you'll learn how to improve the quality of your worship experience, and in so doing, support your efforts to engage members beyond church walls with faith sharing. Your list of tasks is in the chart on the right.

The to-dos on this list lead to a higher-quality worship experience when you take them on. The most essential quality for a church's worship development is the binding focus on faith sharing beyond church walls: being a disciple who makes disciples. You will help increase worship quality by communicating discipleship to your people before, during, and after worship gatherings. Messaging is broken down into two areas:

- small comments you make about worship during worship, and
- sermon preparation during the week.

The "one to many weeks" timeline indicates you can start improving worship dynamics quickly and continue developing them over time.

11. Worship leader dynamics

It's incumbent upon church leaders to help members identify themselves as worship leaders. If you didn't grasp what you read, go back and reread it.

Helping members see themselves as worship leaders is not a magic bullet for growth. It won't automatically change how people perceive themselves within the gathered community. But it will help. It will be a piece of how you create some consistency in your efforts as church leaders to help members begin to move beyond church walls with their own faith. You'll also have to help people see how to improve worship quality, which is driven by outreach to impact community development. Joy is a significant factor in that. Joy will come through outreach by those whose identity is transforming before your very eyes. God is doing the transformation. God will use the transformation of members to influence new people and other members. God wants to be involved in your worship! Your engagement is key to that happening. It won't happen if worship is tepid.

Spend some time reviewing the "Worship quality list." Review public statements you can make to help members begin to see themselves as worship leaders or come up with your own. Write them down.

12. Space dynamics

Many small churches meet in spaces that seat over 150, sometimes up to 250. However, only 20 to 50 people are in attendance. That's not a good ratio, and it will harm you if you're trying to reach new people. If that describes your church, you do not have "critical mass." One of the implications of critical mass is that you have enough people in the right space for your mission field so that the size of the room doesn't dwarf the size of the gathering. New people will enter a space that is too large for the gathering and want to walk right back out. It's called the cringe factor.

You must be aware of that. More on this dynamic in chapter 5.

Critical mass, or its lack, shapes how participants interact with the music and various parts of the worship service. Worship participants will feel more like a community if you can find a way to shrink the room or meet elsewhere in your building. In the opening coaching story called "Mainline Church," the room could seat sixty, and many weeks they had about fifty. However, they could rearrange the seating so that thirty-five people would be comfortable as well. The word *connected* comes to mind.

Pause to consider these thoughts.

- Shrinking your room. Put up artistic dividers or banners you design and have made, usually inexpensively. You can move them around to improve seating options while simultaneously blocking the view of the rest of the room.
- Move your meeting spot. You could move your gathering to a chapel, a library, or a fellowship hall. That could require some outstanding creativity if you have an organist and no organ in the fellowship hall. Who would? There are options to fix that without installing a new organ or losing the organ sound. What do you think those are?

Don't make changes to where you meet just yet, especially if the change would be as drastic as relocating your meeting within the same building. Do wait until at least the end of this chapter, if not the end of chapter five to pursue the conversation.

- Assess the space dynamics for your church. How do you compare to the description? What can you do to make the space more welcoming and worshipful for both regulars and newcomers? Make a list. Consider scheduling a future date to implement some changes. Write down your date and a list of people who need to be involved in the discussion.

13. Flow dynamics

Flow is how each part of the service "flows" into the next. How you have your service organized will help or hinder up-front leaders from expressing themselves. When an up-front worship leader connects with the worship flow, it's easier for them to engage personally in the worship experience and, therefore, to engage with persons in the seats.

Numbers also affect the dynamics of flow because the way you connect with people seated in a smaller venue is different from that in a larger one. The need for technology is generally lower in smaller venues and with smaller audiences. If you're meeting in a large venue with a small number of attendees, you're likely overusing technology.

In a smaller venue with fewer people, the worship leader is usually physically closer to the people in the seats. A larger environment in a modern church, for example, could have a stage and multiple large screens. It's important to remember both the service's organization and the number of people you're leading, as both affect the flow of worship.

But the primary focus of worship flow is typically the sequence of your worship service.

Below are two charts. The one on the left is a traditional church, and the one on the right is more modern. The traditional church has fewer than one hundred, while the contemporary church has more than one hundred. You could reverse the description, so the modern church is the lower number, and the traditional church is the larger one. The point will be primarily to see that the services aren't that different.

Take a look at the chart on the following page, discuss the points outlined there, and talk about your church specifically, then read the analysis that follows.

What to notice about the charts:

- The five headings. These are bolded italics. These are the five parts of worship that guide most public worship gatherings. You can discern what to put under each heading. The headings provide structure. That's freeing, as they're somewhat theological and instructive for those who might resist worship changes. Standing and sitting. Flow is impacted by standing, sitting, and lighting, which isn't featured in the above charts. Electronics and people movement become transitions.

- Use of video. Videos add a lot of dimensions to a service. It's a form of communication that draws people in. You can make them or buy them. You have room for a testimonial video in your weekly worship service. Videos are excellent transition formats. They work in traditional and modern settings.

- Joys and concerns. This area of many traditional services is not represented in either worship format, although the interactive confessional prayer that follows the message is a modern-day form of sharing them. See the next insert for more on this topic, and phase 4 in part II, entry 31.

GATHERING: Pre-service, up to 10 minutes	GATHERING: Pre-service, up to 10 minutes
Announcement reel with background music	Announcement reel with background music
Procession of acolytes	Band enters
People stand	People stand
Formal call to worship	Invitation to sing and praise God
PRAISE: Start of service, 15 minutes	**PRAISE: Start of service, 15. Minutes**
2-3 hymns or hymns and a song	2-3 modern songs and modernized hymns
People sit	People sit
Psalm or lectionary suggested reading	60-second video of the church in mission
Welcome by the pastor or host (3 minutes)	Welcome by a host (3 minutes)
Pray	Pray
PROCLAMATION: 35 minutes	**PROCLAMATION: 35 minutes**
Read scripture or show a testimonial video	Video of scripture or testimonial video
Children's message, kids dismissed	
Choir anthem	Some type of art expression (eg. Original poem)
Preacher message	Preacher message
RESPONSE: 5 minutes	**RESPONSE: 5 minutes**
Interactive, confessional prayer	Interactive, confefssional prayer
DISMISSAL: 1 minute	**DISMISSAL: 1 minute**

If you plan to include joys and concerns, place them toward the end of the service. If you have joys and concerns too early, it can harm your influence, as new people can't relate to what is often a members-only activity. Don't make any sudden moves to change joys and concerns. Read entry 31 first, and the next chapter about conflict.

- Create your own chart to see how your worship flows. Start with the five headings: "Gathering," "Praise," "Proclamation," "Response," "Dismissal." Then put what you already do under each heading. Add in transitions. Consider how everything flows.
- Who do you need to include in a flow conversation?

14. Confessional (Interactive) Prayer

For six years, I worked for the brilliant Martha Grace Reese, JD, MDiv. Gay, the nickname she goes by, designed and led the only major study on evangelism in the mainline church, funded by the Lily Endowment. She titled her research, subsequent books, and teaching series "Unbinding the Gospel."[1]

Gay uncovered many truths about evangelism. One of them is the connection between outreach and prayer. Gay says this: "The heart of evangelism emerges from the interaction of these three sets of relationships: our personal relationships with God, healthy congregational relationships, and caring about people who don't have a conscious connection with Christ."[2]

Prayer is how we communicate with God. It's confessional by nature. When people pray for themselves in their own voice about something they care about, they're much more open to praying for people they know and then those they don't know—and mean it when they do. This type of prayer differs significantly from the prayers of confession written out in the bulletin that we all recite together. There's a place for those prayers, but they don't take the place of personal confession in "my own voice" about "my own life."

How to develop a confessional, interactive prayer for the worship gathering

In evangelism-oriented churches, you'll see laypersons at meetings and gatherings praying out loud in front of the group while their pastors are there, and the pastors are participating in silence as the parishioner leads the prayer. Such prayers are spontaneous and not written out. The only way to teach a congregation to pray in that way is to pray in that way every time you gather.

And to introduce confessional, interactive prayer in worship. After the message is an ideal time to offer a confessional prayer. Making the prayer interactive (not written in the bulletin and recited by the gathered community) engages many people. Including a confessional prayer after the message and toward the end of the service helps to lift the personal nature of prayer. If members can learn to pray using their own voice, it will change the climate of your worship environment. To tie prayer to your message, follow the outline below. As you do, note the overarching sequence, to pray for myself, for someone I know, and for someone I don't know. Memorize that sequence and let it seep in to whatever you do to develop a confessional, interactive prayer approach that's authentic:

A. Prayers for me

  a. Pursue a sermon topic.

    i. One example of a sermon topic could be "Parents Struggling with Parenting."

    ii. Parenting is a common topic in many emerging mission fields, making it a good example to use in a written demo to make it seem more relatable.

    iii. It could be finances, faith, racism, betrayal—all topics can serve as a launchpad for confessional, interactive prayer.

  b. Articulate a central point in your message.

i. One possible main point of a sermon on parenting could be that parents need self-esteem, which comes from God.

c. Ask worshippers to respond to a question by filling in the blank.

i. The question has arisen from the main point.

ii. The question will be fill-in-the-blank.

iii. An example of such a question based on the main point could be:

iv. "I noticed when I didn't respect myself in raising my kids ______________________."

Or

v. "I wish I'd had more self-respect when ______________________________."

vi. Put the fill-in-the-blank question on the screen

d. Direct worshippers to text their response.

i. Include a phone number with the fill-in-the-blank question.

ii. It can be to a texting app or something like it.

e. Play music softly while worshippers are texting and read responses aloud as they come in.

i. Assure worshippers that their texts are anonymous, and you won't know who is saying what.

ii. Or it's possible to utilize a program that sends texts directly to the screen, also anonymously.

f. End this segment with a pastoral prayer.

B. Prayers for those I know

a. Remind worshippers that they have people in their lives who have struggled with (in this case) parenting.

i. Keep the music playing softly.

ii. Ask worshippers to think about someone they know who has struggled with parenting and self-esteem, and pray for their godly self-esteem.

b. Have worshippers say the name of their person silently.

i. Give them about five seconds.

C. Prayers for those I don't know

a. Remind worshippers that many in the neighborhood have trouble with parenting.

b. Offer a prayer for the neighborhood and their godly self-esteem.

i. Give worshippers about ten seconds to think about the neighborhood beyond the church.

c. End with a prayer of gratitude for God listening to everyone's voice.

- Consider the message from last week. What was the main point of the message? What would have been a good open-ended question to ask worshippers to engage with by filling in a blank?
- If you're meeting as a group, experiment with your response to the above bullet. Have members text their response to you and read them as they come in. It won't be anonymous in that setting, but it will be during public worship.
- When might you consider incorporating this type of prayer into your church's worship services?

15. Sermon prep community

Confessional, interactive prayer is an incredible tool for teaching prayer to a congregation and for raising belief in the power of prayer for individuals in the pews. It also utilizes the one voice of the gathered community praying the same thing at the same time (Romans 15:6).

The problem you will encounter in implementing a confessional, interactive prayer that builds on your message is finding two key elements: a clear, central point of your message and a question that engages worshippers and prompts them to respond. The latter is much harder than you think!

The solution is to find a way to engage members and friends in the sermon-prep process. It would involve more than a team because you're not having the same people meet week after week to interact on your message. Instead, you'll gather input from members and guests by reaching out on social media and asking participants to share the main points and questions they've been wrestling with.

Consider the following sequence:

- Post on your preferred platform: What are you struggling with this week? Or what should the church be talking about that we aren't? Or what is one thing about parenting you wish you had known when you first became a parent? Or have you ever had trouble with parenting (or finances, or betrayal, etc.)? Please email me directly.
- Follow up with those who respond directly and perhaps offline (depending on the sensitivity of the topic) by saying: What is the one thing you want to know about (the topic you're interacting on)?
- Now you have a topic and the makings of a fill-in-the-blank question.
- You can go back to members you trust and run things by them and even sit down with a couple of people over coffee to ask them for help in clarifying your point and coming up with a fill-in-the-blank question.
- You can do something like this every week—if you're organized enough to work at least a few weeks ahead of the topic you're researching.
- What social media platforms does your church use? Start there by calendaring when you'll put out a feeler to gauge participant interaction. Don't be deterred by an initial lack of engagement from your followers. Consider working with someone in your church who understands how best to utilize various platforms or find someone in the mission field who will guide you and calendar when you're going to pursue your process.

Rewriting your story reflection questions

1. Say why and how what you just read was:
    - surprising,
    - engaging,
    - confusing,
    - encouraging, or
    - concerning.
2. Where did you see your church in what you read?
3. Where did you see yourself?

4. Who were you thinking about in what you just read?

5. Additional chapter questions:
    - How are you seeing prayer practices and disciplines expanded in this chapter from the first chapter?
    - What outcome do you long for by introducing more prayer in your church?

6. What are you going to do next?

Chapter Postscripts

Going online

Pastoral leaders need to engage with social media, but doing so is often very difficult for them. The Church of the Resurrection (COR) has resources available. Use those, and the resources in this material too.

See the posting schedule outlined in part II, phase 3, entry #20.

Developing an online faith community is an integral part of outreach efforts. Fast-forward to chapter 5 if you'd like to read more about developing an online faith community now.

Developing a sermon series on worship

If you offer an annual sermon series on worship, you can tie participation in this study of rebuilding in-person worship to it. Scan the QR code at the back of this book for a free download including how to learn more about putting together such a series.

Starting a service with a different style

When a worship gathering is "maxed out," you'll find it's time to start another gathering, perhaps with a different style. Being maxed out means you have too many people in your worship space, and you need to add another gathering. It also means that you've grown more diverse and can no longer include enough new things in that service to reach an entirely new mission field. One of the most powerful realities of engaging new people in worship through faith sharing is that it produces diversity. Develop your new style for a new mission field by using the same process you've used to pursue faith sharing beyond church walls.

Fast-forward to leading worship

For further insight into worship leading, jump ahead to part II, entry #31: "Update in-person worship with spiritual practices."

You can deepen the worship experience by including worship leading as described in this entry. The entry is in part II because it may be too much for some churches to undertake at this time. However, it will be essential to increase worship leading in this way by the time you reach part II and this specific entry; if you can incorporate it now, all the better.

Chapter Three

EXPECTING PUSHBACK

Chapter Notes

In a word, this chapter will be familiar. I've never coached a church through worship and outreach without having to deal with conflict. What could be different, though, is seeing the conflict as a deepening experience for the church and bringing it out in mission rather than ignoring or burying it. Use it to lead into confession, forgiveness, and the pursuit of faith beyond the building. If you're looking for authenticity, that's how you'll find it.

Chapter Notes reflection question:

What is your expectation of this chapter?

I. Real-Life Coaching Stories

Triangulation One: Pastor, people, new people

Early in my coaching ministry, a client had a parishioner show up unannounced when the pastor, my client, was not there. The pastor had been summoned by the fire department for a grandfather and granddaughter living together whose home had just burned to the ground. The two occupants escaped, safe. When the fire chief asked the residents if they had a church, they said that this was their church and that was their pastor. The pastor had no idea who they were! But when he got there, he recognized the granddaughter from a couple of youth events. He ministered to the family and initiated the process for the church to assist them. When he got back to his office, he found a note on the door from the woman who had dropped in unannounced. She was steamed! He wasn't there! She knew where he was because the church admin had told her. The angry woman's closing line in the poison-pen letter the pastor found on the door was "Pastor, you know those people are not members." Signed, (member name).

It was just one member, but others agreed with her. And there were yet others who didn't. For those who did, it was like they saw the new people as "the enemy" coming between them and their shepherd. The pastor wasn't going to let that dynamic go. I was proud of him!

Triangulation Two: Pastor, individuals

The pastor of the wealthy, smaller church had posted his office hours on the office door. When he returned late one day from a personal errand, the hours were ripped off the door and crumpled on the floor. It reminded me of the time when my other client had received a poison-pen note on his door from a parishioner for not being there when she dropped in because he was out ministering to victims of a fire. That pastor wasn't angry for himself. He was offended on behalf of the fire victims. At first, I thought this pastor had the same right to holy indignation as the first pastor, because the parishioner expected the pastor to be there for them.

But I'm not sure that the anger was exactly justified. You'd think that the pastor would have been less drawn into the parishioner's blatant acting out, which was more childish than toxic. There was bad blood between the members and the pastor because he instituted many worship changes when he first arrived, without working through any change dynamics. No one liked what he did. They had stopped serving on their committees and had started openly expressing their anger toward the pastor. I wasn't hired to work through conflict with them. I was hired to help the pastor start a new worship service. That wasn't going to work, given their conflict.

We discussed the possibility of the pastor meeting with the board chairperson over the crumpled paper. The board chairperson probably already knew what had happened since it was a small, ingrown church, and the board chairperson knows everything! If the pastor had gone to the board chairperson in humility to ask him not to reveal who it was, but to speak to the person, apologizing to the person on the pastor's behalf, it could have opened the door to greater transparency and honesty. The pastor wouldn't be creating a triangle. The triangle was already in existence. The board chairperson could encourage the person to go directly to the pastor so the pastor could also apologize in person. That would have benefited the pastor in leading change, which he said he wanted to do, but didn't act like it.

As an introvert, the pastor needed time to process. He returned to coaching, saying he'd do nothing. That was the beginning of the end of his tenure. It was predictable.

Triangulation Three: Pastor, staff, mission

When a church hires me for consulting, it's common for staff to feel nervous. We can mostly get beyond that. The coach will encourage the pastor to set up the role of the outsider (the coach) and to process with the pastor what to say so that staff don't feel too threatened. But you never know exactly what the pastor says or the actual dynamics between the pastor and staff until you begin working with them. I've found that some pastors even of larger churches with a worship attendance approaching 250 can have an unhealthy closeness with staff, especially when the staff is about the size of a small group. One possible reason is that the pastor is struggling with the congregation's growth. Leadership is lonely. Pastors can become enmeshed with the captive audience (the staff). The coach discovers the enmeshment when the pastor comes to coaching one day to tell you that the staff didn't like what you said. When you probe to find out why, it turns out the pastor didn't like what you said and told the staff in a way that made the staff want to protect the pastor, whom they wanted to please. On the surface, it looks like the pastor is creating a triangle between the staff and the coach. But really, the triangle is between the pastor, the staff, and the church's mission, since enmeshment is an ingrown behavior. The overly close relationship between the pastor and the staff will impede their ability to see what's working and what's not to reach their target. That's a challenging coaching situation because the pastor must see what s-he has done in creating the triangle, then be willing to confess it to the staff, ask for forgiveness, and not repeat it. It's the not-repeating-it part that's hard, because the pastor must set boundaries that separate the pastor from the staff so the pastor can't use the staff for personal reasons. That's a significant and disruptive shift from an existing dynamic.

Triangulation Four: Pastor, musicians, vacuum

Sometimes an organist or choir director of a tiny church will reach out to me independent of the pastor to ask why the church needs to change, and why worship needs to change "when the members like it." The musician's actions and words are a powerful display of institutionalism. The musician wants to talk with me about the pastor and create a problem with the pastor. If you're going to keep a church small, you'll try to make a triangle that's built upon gossip or backtalk. I've learned not to respond to the email right away, then loop back around to tell the musician something like, *"This would be a good conversation to have with your pastor."*

But my issue isn't so much with the musician as it is with the pastor, who has no idea what the musician is doing or thinking. Yet the pastor has included the musician in teaching and coaching, which is how the musician got my contact information. Pastors must learn to read the room. When they don't, it harms the process of worship development. Many musicians dig in their heels when faced with the need to improve what they do in worship. They take it personally because artists consider their work an extension of themselves. Pastors need to speak with musicians about their heart for worship as a first step before asking them to be part of a study that examines worship, just because they're musicians. By ignoring the heart of the musician, the pastor has created a void in which all sorts of trouble can emerge.

Triangulation Five: Mission, parishioner, parishioner's friend

One client came to a coaching session once to tell me about a board member weeping at a board meeting over all the changes the church was going through. The pastor suggested they go for coffee after the meeting. The pastor knew part of the change the board member was talking about concerned his friend, who had left the church to find another church. She and her family didn't like all the changes, and they were angry at the board member for sticking around. The board member was still on board with where the church was going, but wished he'd been able to help his friend and her family change their minds. But the layperson had no training and didn't recognize grief. And now he was identifying his own grief. In a broad sense, the grief is like a third person in a congregation that has growing pains: the church, the mission, and the emotional reactions. Members need guidance for handling their grief. If a church leader can help members recognize their own emotions, worship increases as God's power for healing takes root.

Coaching stories reflection questions:

- What points did the stories raise?
- Did any describe you or your church? How?

II. Backstories of Institutionalism

Insights into the opening stories

Triangulation is a familiar dynamic in churches. Leaders have a big part in either diffusing or promoting triangulation. That's the gist of all the opening stories.

But triangulation is not really the point of introducing those stories. Instead, it's the system that supports the triangulation that is important to see. Ministry is both a profession and a calling that evokes strong emotions. We get involved, and it goes to the deepest part of us. When things get difficult in the faith community, it's bound to elicit anger and the tendency to control and act out. We're only human. But in the institutional (and sometimes toxic) church, the tendency to act out is collective, not just individual. The collective nature of rebellion is greater than the sum of the parts. It has its own power. If you can't or won't see the pull of negativity, you'll succumb to it. Most church leaders succumb to it, but they don't have to. It is challenging work not to succumb, and we're up to the task if we let God lead us into the mission field to share faith. Mission is the primary reason to pursue conflict with members without hiding it or running away from it. That changes the system. Changing the system increases worship.

Systems

We've identified a systems conversation. I'm not a systems expert. However, I've been around church systems long enough to make some observations regarding institutionalism in the church. An institutional system has a strong pull to stay inwardly focused. When a church takes on an outward focus, the inwardly concentrated side of the church will try to stop you. The system itself will pull you back. Pastors and parishioners alike are vulnerable to that pull. I'll share a personal story to illustrate.

The metaphor of the mobile

My sister was a chronic alcoholic. She passed away when I was in seminary from alcohol-related illness. A seminary professor suggested that I take a class in which I could participate as an observer during family week at a local treatment center. It was my first exposure to treatment. Family week is when the family of the identified patient (the one undergoing treatment) participates in the treatment process and learns to recognize their own role in the family's disease. Yes, chemical dependency is a family disease. We all have a part in furthering the dependency until we learn how not to.

A counselor in recovery gave a powerful talk that week. She used the image of a mobile to describe the family system plagued by chemical dependency. The artsy mobile you hang from your ceiling has several arms arranged to balance it. If you take one arm off, the mobile becomes unbalanced. To rebalance the mobile, a new arm or the replacement of the old arm is required. Or you could completely redesign the mobile with existing parts. The mobile can't right itself.

The family is a system. When the identified patient pursues health, the family can flounder because one of the arms is gone. They're going to work overtime to get the arm back by repeating the behavior that goes with the old system, even if the family wants the identified patient to get well. The hope is that, when the family changes their behavior, the identified patient is free to pursue life a day at a time. Otherwise, the identified patient is between a rock and a hard place. They can succumb to the pull of the family disease and give up their health journey, or they can fully unhook their arm and reject their family in favor of health.

Explaining and applying the metaphor of the mobile to the church

You can apply the same dynamic of the out-of-balance mobile to the church when a leader, typically the pastor, undertakes personal outreach in the neighborhood. Not many members will initially understand outreach as the doorway to worship development because of their ties to the existing institutional system. That makes the pastor or leader and the layperson who is an early adopter of worship changes vulnerable. An unhealthy system will always try to pull a key leader back into unhealthy behavior that fosters institutionalism. You can be a willing participant with your own bad behavior by allowing a knee-jerk reaction to dictate what you do, or you can develop faith. The latter is much harder and the more enduring choice.

Fear and Trembling

The faith and courage required for a leader to lead a church in fighting the tendency to remain institutional are immense. Getting out into the secular culture to talk about faith is a new behavior for a church and its leaders. It causes stress and disruption to the perfectly balanced institutional system. Trusting God to keep your eyes focused on outreach, therefore, is also the solution, or the treatment that rebalances the system. Believing that God is the one who's driving this process is what rebuilds the system. It's not so easy because of what *could* be: failure. If you trust God, though, it is always success, even when it may appear to be failure.

The kind of faith and trust we're talking about shows up in the story of Abraham and Isaac in Genesis 22. Abraham brings his son Isaac to the altar to possibly sacrifice him to God in death. Isaac was God's promise to Abraham to live on through the generations—Abraham's beloved son. If Abraham loses Isaac to death, what will happen to Abraham's legacy? Many interpretations of this story suggest that Abraham was a man of obedience, as he brought Isaac to the altar, despite the possibility of losing his lineage. That interpretation implies that Christ's followers need to be obedient to God. That obedience could be described as "blind faith."

Søren Kierkegaard offers a different interpretation of Genesis 22 in his treatise, *Fear and Trembling*. It's an intense read, and I hope I'm doing it justice with this short synopsis. Kierkegaard paints Abraham as a man of faith, not obedience. Kierkegaard concludes that if Abraham were a man of obedience, he'd be a tragic figure. Whatever happened would have happened *to* him. God would take Isaac or release Isaac, and Abraham would not have had any input. His faith would have been blind before what could be considered a capricious god. Thus, Abraham is a man of faith who isn't blind. His eyes are wide open. He fully trusts the most perfect God to take Isaac and, at the same time, fully trusts God to save Isaac. Whatever happens will be right because Abraham deeply trusts God, trusting in God's will and truth. Therefore, Abraham is a participant in the outcome, not a victim of it. His faith will lead him to cope with whatever truth God reveals.

Powers and principalities

Ephesians 6:12 (CEB) says: "We aren't fighting against human enemies but against rulers, authorities, forces of cosmic darkness, and spiritual powers of evil in the heavens."If your church and your leadership want to grow fully trusting of God, no matter the outcome, then somewhere along the line, you must recognize that the issues you're fighting against aren't the issues. Can you do that? It's a byproduct of sharing faith beyond church walls. It's going to disrupt people, and that will further engage your surrender and passion. If you bring those dynamics to worship, things will change.

Some mainliners don't like to think about good and evil, and powers and principalities. However, it is there in the Bible. I'm okay with finding any way you can to learn to deal with the pushback that always arises when you pursue a mission. Two steps forward, one step back.

That said, if you can come to terms with the language of good and evil, it will be compelling and modern. I'm not a gamer, but it seems many video games build on the good-versus-evil dichotomy. Or maybe you're a Marvel comic devotee. Marvel movies and many modern television series feature archetypal characters. You do not have to be a Christian charismatic or an evangelist to understand that sometimes evil is present and that it can take over some people, and that good exists to overcome evil. Church leaders can identify evil in the body without blame so that members can see how tempting it is. Now, when you worship God as a community of disciples, worship takes on even greater meaning.

And then, in seven years, when you see the whole fruit of culture change, you'll be able to look back and know how much your faith community let go of their old ways in favor of their surrender. That's the good news and a description of your future longevity as a faith community if you discern that this is the route you should take.

Backstories reflection questions

1. Say why what you just read was:
   - surprising,
   - engaging,
   - confusing,
   - encouraging, or
   - concerning.
2. Where did you see your church in what you read?
3. Where did you see yourself?
4. Who were you thinking about in what you just read?
5. What are you going to do next?

III. Rewriting Your Church's Story

You may notice that the charts are getting shorter. There aren't as many new entries in the following chart as there were in the previous one. Additionally, you're continuing to implement the changes introduced in the earlier columns, which still impact your current timeline in the new chapter you're in. Suppose you have free time because there aren't as many tasks to do this time as there were before. If you're done with all the other stuff from the previous columns, use your time to deepen the discussion about conflict and systems. Seeing the dynamics is a game changer in learning to be an outwardly focused church. Consider this question: What is the most disruptive part of this chapter so far and how are you going to deal with it?

Expecting Pushback
16. Gather intercessors 17. Pursue Mt. 18 18. Come to Jesus 19. Preach on conflict 20. Do prayer walks
One month to many weeks

16. Gather Intercessors

When you approach prayer with focus and intentionality, the need for intercession becomes apparent. Developing intercessors enables you to build more effective systems.

When members push back against outreach practices, the appropriate response is often for the pastor to have a come-to-Jesus conversation with the resistor. That conversation is not to be taken lightly. It can be dramatic for everyone. No one knows the outcome. It's not always a given that the pastor will survive such drama. Some churches are toxic. Members will gang up against the pastor if they don't like what the pastor is doing. They'll go over the pastor's head to complain about the pastor. Have the come-to-Jesus conversation about what a Christian really is, but lay groundwork with personal intercessors first:

"But Moses' hands grew tired. So they took a stone and put it under Moses so he could sit down on it. Aaron and Hur held up his hands, one on each side of him so that his hands remained steady until sunset" (Exodus 17:12).

How to gather intercessory prayer support:

- Sit in silence. Ask God for the names of people who would be willing to intercede for you.
- Find support not from your church. Most of the battles will be with people from your church. It puts a stumbling block in front of even the most faithful members when you need prayer from them because one of their friends is misbehaving.
- Ask God for a dozen names. They won't all say yes.
- Pray over the list. Eliminate some names.
- Pray over the list again. Eliminate more names until you have five to seven names remaining.
- Send the following email:
  Dear (friend), I need some people to pray for me because I'm starting to do the work of outreach in my church. I may occasionally reach out to you with a specific prayer request. If I do, I'll send you an update that's about as long as this email. So you don't have to read a bunch of stuff that only I care about! Sometimes I'd hope you'd pray for me as God brings me to mind. Pray for whatever you think I need prayer for. I'm thinking this need will last about the next six months. Are you in?
- Expect some people to say no. They know prayer is work, and they can't do it right now.
- Keep your promise. Send short prayer requests and short emails, and don't check in much beyond that, except at the six-month point.
- Regroup at six months. Check in with your intercessors to see whether they still want to pray for you or would prefer you find someone else.
- Laypersons follow this process. Dedicated laypersons in outreach development also need personal intercessors.
- Try praying and making a list of possible intercessors. Write down the date when you're going to reach out to them.

17. Pursue Matthew 18 (a conflict resolution process)

Most small churches lack a mechanism to address conflicts that compromise their health and missional purpose. The most straightforward approach is to pursue Matthew 18.

I saw Matthew 18 in action at the megachurch where I served. A member was not taking her medicine for bipolar disease and was disruptive during in-person worship. The church went through a year-long process with the member that ultimately led to her "eviction." Could you do that for the sake of the mission? You will need a lot of reinforcements if you do. You can trust that somewhere along the line, there will be a member who will be so disruptive and will want to see you fail that you'll need to address the disruption head-on. If you don't, the toxicity will overtake your church, and you'll decline further.

- How does your church's conflict resolution process work? Does it revolve around Matthew 18? Do you even have one? What resources are available to help you develop one? By what date do you want to have something like this in place? Write it down.

18. Come to Jesus

Considering intercessory prayer support and a Matthew 18 process, we'll demo and otherwise discuss a come-to-Jesus approach for each of the opening coaching stories. You'll notice the stories have new titles. The latest title indicates a potential new ending to the story.

Opening Story One: Following a Plan for Health

(Setting: the pastor invited the parishioner to his office)

Pastor: Bonnie, good to see you.

Bonnie: Thank you, Pastor. I wasn't sure you were interested!

Pastor: Well, I got your note. You got my attention!

Bonnie: Yes, well, I don't think it's right for you to be out with people who don't come to this church and who don't tithe.

Pastor: Oh. Well, I don't think you tithe, do you?

Bonnie: Well, no. But I give money, and we members pay your salary.

Pastor: Right. How does your paying my salary equate with my not caring for someone in need who isn't as visible in the church as you are?

Bonnie: Because God wants us members to be taken care of.

Pastor: Hmm. I'm not so sure about that. I've always known God to want us to take the time to minister to people when they're suffering, which these folks were, and maybe even to tell them about Jesus.

Bonnie: So you don't think you should be taking care of us as your first priority?

Pastor: I don't.

Bonnie: I know the people you were with. They're not like the rest of us here.

Pastor: What do you mean by that?

Bonnie: Well, I just think you could help them find another church.

Pastor: Funny you should say that. They said we were their church.

Bonnie: Well, I think if you told anyone on the board that you were with these people, they'd say what I said.

Pastor: I did talk to Randy. He seemed very concerned about the grandfather's well-being. He knows him from the VFW.

Bonnie: (silent)

Pastor: Bonnie, when I was growing up, I was an outcast. I'm a nerd, you know? Kids didn't like me very well. I had to grow out of that lack of self-esteem. Following Jesus helped me. My wife is a music nerd. We make a good pair, don't you think?

Bonnie: You do.

Pastor: But the rejection of the kids growing up still stings when I think about it.

Bonnie: What is your point?

Pastor: Well, as the church we have a chance to do something different for this family you don't seem to want here.

Bonnie: I didn't say I didn't want them.

Pastor: What did you say then?

Bonnie: I said I didn't think they'd fit in.

Pastor: That's where we're different. Jesus will help them fit in.

Bonnie: Maybe I'll be the one to leave.

Pastor: Bonnie, you don't have to do that, although if that's what you want to do I can't stop you.

Bonnie: You see? I told you I'm not that important to you.

Pastor: I can't take sides to prefer you over a new person, Bonnie. That's not what Christianity is. I would much rather help you help them. You could be such a light in their lives if you learned to care for them and others who might be different.

Bonnie: I'm a good person!

Pastor: You are, indeed, Bonnie. There are so many things about you that are great that could be so beneficial to someone else who is seeking faith. I'd really like to help you do that.

Bonnie: I'm not going to sit here and be insulted. I'm going to go to Randy and tell him the board should think about replacing you. I'm going to write to your supervisor.

Pastor: You have that right, Bonnie. In fact, let's set up a meeting with Randy, you, and me to start. Maybe we can work something out. If not, we'll invite my supervisor to be part of the conversation.

What does the new title mean?

Opening Story Two: Loving People Enough to Be Humble

Leaving an appointment or call to a church in which there is hidden conflict is perhaps the only solution that remains if the leader is unwilling to take the plunge in coming to Jesus. But even if the leader is willing to take that plunge, the leader may still be forced out. There are no guarantees that conflict resolution and truth-telling will favor the leader or the church's mission. The leader must be ready to withstand the pressure of pushback. Some leaders aren't. If the leader loves the people, the leader will give up their position to allow someone else with the skills for clarity work with them, or the leader will be willing to lose their own position should it come to that when the leader pursues truth-telling. The pastor who loves the people enough to confront control and anger has a lot of humility. One way to address conflict openly is to preach about it.

What would you say in a sermon that addressed the conflict of this church from the opening story? Write some things down before reading the upcoming entry on preaching about conflict (entry 19).

Opening Story Three: Teaching About Systems

When the coach discovers an unhealthy relationship between the pastor and their staff and, simultaneously, the pastor becomes open to seeing the dynamic for themselves, it's time for a teaching moment. This was what it looked like with the pastor in question. We discussed:

1. Triangulating. When the pastor gets cozy with the staff and puts their own insecurities out there for others to assuage, it's called "triangulation." If the pastor is triangulating with the staff, they are likely doing so with the congregation as well. Have you ever seen that in yourself? Why do you think that's happening?

- The fix: confession that you're looking for the staff (and others) to protect you. Request that your intercessors pray for your personal confession.

2. Asking forgiveness. When the pastor realizes they have created a dependency on the staff who do not want to offend them, the pastor must own it. What could you say to your staff to let them know you have gone in an unhelpful direction with them? It doesn't need to be much.

    - The fix: Ask forgiveness of those who depend on you, then promise not to create that dependency again. Request your intercessors pray for your courage to avoid any further triangulations.

3. Going direct. Sometimes the staff has legitimate concerns about the direction of outreach and worship. The pastor must be able to distinguish between legitimate concerns and gossip. Was there anything that I said that we need to work out with your staff? Can we set up a conversation?

    - The fix. When the pastor hears staff concerns about various worship directions and they are directed at a specific person, the pastor sets up a conversation among the staff, the pastor, and the other person. Request your intercessors to pray for that meeting while it's happening.

What confessions might you need to make about triangulation?

Opening Story Four: Letting Go of Your Art

In the previous chapter, we devoted considerable time to discussing the quality of the worship experience. No matter how much you pray or how kind you are in talking with your musicians and artists about worship quality, they're still likely to be defensive. You can work through that, but it might take some time. Keep the focus on the mission and be clear about what the mission is. Reassure the musician that they're a great artist. Help them see that their art is a gift from God that they are being asked to share. Engaging the musician on how they want to live out their mission and legacy through their music will be helpful. What do they think about people who don't know Jesus? How can the church engage them? How is everything going now?

Having your intercessors praying while you're pursuing the conversation is a must! What can't happen is for a musician or anyone else to try to control what your church does by being personally negative, triangulating, or drawing a line in the sand about what they're willing to do for the church, or not. If your musician does any of those things, you'll need a larger strategy.

Is there a deeper conversation in your future between the pastor and the musician in your church to talk about the mission of the church and the mission of the artist?

Opening Story Five: Just Between Friends

Gina: Hey Rod! What did you think of pastor's sermon today.
Rod: I thought it was courageous.
Gina: That outreach stuff isn't for me. I was raised to be reserved about my faith.
Rod: I know. But you can change that.
Gina: I'm not going to go around hounding people.
Rod: Where did you get the idea that you're hounding people?
Gina: You have to pray and get together and pray and talk and see if the person wants to do something with the church. . . . I don't need that kind of time commitment.

Rod: (Silently, "God, give the words and the heart right now.")
Gina I don't get the big deal. Why does anyone need to hear personal details about my life?
Rod: Do you mean your faith story?
Gina: Yes. I've just always been a Christian.
Rod: So then you have a ton of faith to share with others.
Gina: think it's BS.
Rod: Why do you feel so threatened?
Gina: Why do you think I feel threatened?
Rod: Because you don't want to talk about your life.
Gina: It's my life. It's private.
Rod: Well, I can see that. But it seems like you'd have a lot to share to help someone else grow.
Gina: It's just hard for me to see how anything I have to say is going to help someone else grow.
Rod: I kind of get that. But I think it could. I'll say this. I think this is probably the future of the church. And that's a lot of change for us old-timers to have to endure.
Gina: So you think the reason I'm upset is all the change we're dealing with?
Rod: I'm just wondering if that isn't part of it. I feel that way personally. I just think that our church is probably not going to make it unless we do something drastic like this.
Gina: Maybe not. I just don't know if I'm ready for it. You know Jerry isn't going to go for it.
Rod: So let's you and Jerry and me get together and figure it out.
Gina: Wanna come for dinner?
Rod: Sure.

What kind of support does your congregation need over grief and grieving, considering worship changes?

19. Preach on Conflict

The example of the pastor who preached about conflict in his church on the day I visited that church is worth rereading, in chapter 2, Opening Coaching Story One: Fun Church. Consider how much went into developing that message.

If the pastor/preacher/leader were a true leader, he wouldn't go it alone when developing his message. Likely, he spoke with his board or lead team, specific lay leaders, and possibly a denominational supervisor, depending on the denominational structure. In some tribes, the supervisor plays a significant role in church life. It's helpful to inform your supervisor and discuss the public address when you are ready to deliver it, and perhaps even invite them to attend. If you have a good relationship with your supervisor and they are mission-minded, they can speak briefly to the congregation and be available for conversation afterward. Not going it alone also means that your intercessors are in place, and your church is pursuing some conflict-resolution approach that centers around Matthew 18.

In preparing your sermon/message, remember a few things:

- Focus on God's mission for the church.
- Be articulate about how God is leading you personally.
- Speak about life-changing conversations you've had with new people in the mission field.
- Speak about surrender to God's leading of the church.
- Name your worries for the church if the church doesn't pursue mission.
- Speak plainly about what rebelliousness is: rejecting God's will for the church.
- Confess your own rejection of God's will (because you've had it, 100 percent true).

- Offer forgiveness but do not suggest returning to the way things were.
- Name grief.
- Name healing.

- End with the prayer exercise outlined in the previous chapter, "Leading Worship." Engage some members to help you with the fill-in-the-blank question. Here are a few examples of what it could be:
  - o The change that is the most difficult to see in the church is ________________.
  - o The change I wish I could make is ________________________________.
  - o God's purpose for the church is ________________________________.

Is there a need at your church to address conflict publicly? How and when will you do that? What kind of support do you need?

20. Do Prayer Walks.

The most influential way to bring members along in the pursuit of the mission is to help them see the harvest. When church leaders hammer members for not being willing to change, it backfires. When they focus on the church's mission to be a disciple who makes new disciples and then teaches others to do the same, it helps create fertility. Prayer walks are a way to reinforce the church's mission.
Prayer walks are new for most mainliners. Here's how to organize them.

1. Establish goals.
   a. To grow your heart for the mission field
   b. To discern that you know who the mission field is by how your heart feels..
   c. To identify the right leader who will match the mission field
2. Go alone first.
   a. The project leader walks or drives by homes, businesses, farms, schools, and other churches alone to discern where to send others.
   b. Bless those who work or live or attend where you're driving or walking by.
   c. Ask God for insights into their lives.
   d. Pray for healing, encouragement, or other things that come into your heart.
   e. Make observations and write them down, including:
      i. What is in the driveways and front yards?
      ii. The ambience of the neighborhood or business area (thriving, organized, run down)
      iii. Where are the schools and what are the conditions of the schools and playgrounds?
      iv. What do you take any of your observations to mean?
   f. Pray over your notes.

3. Expand the process.
   a. Engage a variety of members in a prayer walk or drive, including:
      i. Board members
      ii. Participants in your eight-week study
      iii. Members at large who want to grow spiritually
   b. Gathering before the prayer walk/drive
      i. Offer a short teaching when you gather
         1. Include insights from your recent solo and group prayer walks.
         2. Teach that partners pray aloud as a conversation so that when others see them walking or driving, it appears normal to the observer.
         3. Do a demo of what a prayer walk would be like with a partner
         4. Prepare a dialogue that shows what people say and do on the walk.
         5. Prepare to disburse into the community two by two.
         6. Preassign pairs based on the list of people you know are participating.
         7. Send each pair out to a four-or-so-block area to walk, or possibly more to drive.
      ii. Prearrange driving or walking routes before your session, and provide maps.
      iii. If you're walking,
         1. Don't stop to pray over each house or business. Just keep walking!
         2. Don't stop to talk to people. You can say hello, but keep walking!
         3. If someone stops you and asks you about yourself (very unlikely), tell them the truth!
   c. Reconvene after you've done approximately forty-five minutes (includes the time it takes to get to your assigned area and return to the church).
      i. Gather back at your original location after you've completed your route.
      ii. Debrief with a scribe (someone to take notes).
      iii. Talk about how God was real during your event.
      iv. Make observations too, like *houses that seemed run down,* or *boats in about 60 percent of the driveways.*
      v. Include some thoughts about how you're using a demographic study to pair with your insights from the prayer walks. See next entry.
      vi. Draw some conclusions about where God might be leading your church based on the combined results of the demographic study and the prayer walks.
      vii. Compile the notes after and make them accessible to participants.
      viii. Schedule another prayer walking event before you leave for the night!

When will you do your first prayer walk? Calendar it. Whom will you bring with you? Make a list and a timeline for engaging participants. How will you speak about the results publicly? Jot down some ideas.

Rewriting Your Church's Story Reflection Questions

1. Say why what you just read was:

    - surprising,
    - engaging,
    - confusing,
    - encouraging, or
    - concerning.

2. Where did you see your church in what you read?

3. Where did you see yourself?

4. Who were you thinking about in what you just read?

5. Additional chapter questions

    - How do you feel about gathering some personal intercessors? Will you do it? Calendar when.
    - How might you pursue come-to-Jesus conversations with members or staff? What might "being careful" mean if it doesn't mean not having the conversation?

6. What are you going to do next?

Chapter Postscript: Writing Your Own Ending

It may benefit you in this chapter to return to the preface to think about what it means to write your own ending to the story of your church. You're overcoming institutionalism. And while the stories in this chapter are universal, they're not necessarily exactly what is going on in your church. To further contextualize the material, you can rewrite the dialogues with your own spin.

Chapter Four

GETTING COMFORTABLE WITH FAITH TALK

Chapter Notes

This chapter is the most practical of all the chapters in part I. That doesn't make it the easiest. However, the act of doing it will reduce its daunting nature. Don't just read it. Do it!

Chapter Notes reflection question

What is your expectation of this chapter?

I. Real-Life Coaching Stories

A Parishioner's Story

I asked the pastor who would be a good person to share a personal faith story during a training session at her church. She sent over a woman I'll call S. I told S to talk about a time in her life when God became real to her. S told the story to the group about the night she almost took the knife lying on the kitchen table to her own heart. She'd been depressed because of a divorce and ensuing financial trouble. Her parents were conservative, and divorce was not condoned. S had two teenage daughters that she was barely supporting—not financially, not emotionally, not holistically. Their dad was estranged too. S felt she had let everyone down. As S picked up the knife, she heard a voice. S had never heard a voice before, and she had never heard the words "You are good, you are mine." S trembled as she broke into tears and the knife dropped from her hand. She had the faintest glimmer of hope. No one in the room, except the pastor and S's new husband, had ever heard that story before. You could hear a pin drop.

A Customer's Story

Between 2022 and 2024, I worked retail at the Mall of America, which is about fifteen minutes from where I live. The general manager of a store where I purchase most of my clothes recruited me. I thought it sounded like fun. It was much more than that as God led me into conversations about faith with people far from God and the church. I'd pray every time I went in for a shift that God would open the doorway to faith talk. Don't pray that prayer if you don't mean it. Some conversations were substantial. I got to learn how people outside the church think about the church. I got to hear how they pursue spirituality beyond church walls. I even sometimes got to say why I follow Jesus.

One day, I was speaking with the customer's partner as I was running outfits back and forth to the customer. The topic of religion came up. I asked the partner if he was a person of faith. Yes, he'd grown up in the church, but now found it so institutional. That was something I heard commonly. I wondered what the man did. He was a surgeon, and his wife was a nurse practitioner. I asked him where he lived. Leawood, Kansas, he replied. I'm chuckling even now at how God seems to line things up. Possibly the most famous United Methodist church in the world is in Leawood, Kansas, and I'm a United Methodist. I asked if he'd ever heard of Church of the Resurrection (COR).

I have never been to COR, but I have heard the founding pastor speak many times and have met a couple of staff members. It would be an excellent place for the doctor and his spouse to see a church that is outreach-oriented, even if it's a megachurch and probably has to fight institutionalism, just like every (mega)church. I told the doctor I struggle with church institutionalism too. I said that I was still a Christ follower, and that my faith in Christ went beyond self-esteem for me. I told him about COR and said I thought he could get questions answered there. He wasn't offended.

A Pastor's Story

It's common for churchgoers to feel they don't have any interesting stories to tell about their own faith. They've been Christ followers their whole lives, and they can't think of a time when they didn't follow Jesus. Fair enough; not everyone has a dramatic story to tell about Jesus becoming real to them. But if you probe with the person who says they've always been a believer, you find a story just the same. That's what you'd call a plot twist: helping the person discover that they have a story to share that will be relevant to other people. I do that in my seminars. Take Pastor N. She was forlorn because she didn't have a story. I started asking her questions. Where did you grow up? How old were you when you remember knowing Jesus? That got her talking! She was seven when a new kid in her school came to live with her grandmother, who was a church friend of Pastor N's mother. The little girl (we'll call her T) was shy and didn't make friends easily. N befriended T, and they became besties. One day, T told N that she was going to see her mom, who was in some place getting help for being sick. N never asked T why she had to live with her grandmother, but she asked her mom when she went home. Her mom just said T's mother was very ill, and then she said, "I'm proud of you for being so kind to T. She has been through a lot. So many kids weren't kind to her. You're so grown up being a friend!" N went to her bedroom right then and knelt by the bedside, praying for T and T's mom. That sense of identity led her to respond with grace to people increasingly throughout her life. I asked Pastor N if any of that felt like a story to her. She said that maybe it was the grace and generosity that she felt made her who she was. I encouraged her to pursue that connecting point with others.

Coaching stories reflection questions

- What points did the stories raise?
- Did any describe you or your church? How?

II. Backstories of Institutionalism

Insights into the opening stories

All the opening coaching stories you just read are about faith stories. They're not faith stories someone is telling you about their own life, in the first person. A faith story is told in the first person. We'll be reframing the opening stories in this way, so that you can learn to tell your own, succinct, and compelling faith story, which the institutional church often prevents you from doing. Church people get excited about telling their stories and include every detail of their lives, even after I have provided clear instructions about length and how to organize their points. If you do that, new people will tune you out. The institutionalism you're exhibiting assumes that they'll care.

Stumbling blocks to writing your testimony

You'll find several barriers to producing the kind of story that translates into sharing faith beyond church walls, including:

1. The elevator pitch. You won't like this language, or the idea that you must be strategic when talking about faith. It's time to surrender! You have about one minute to share your faith story with someone you know well or don't know well. A minute is about how long it takes to ride an elevator down from the top floor of a skyscraper to the first floor without stopping. If you're still talking by the time you get to the ground floor, your person is going to race out to get away from your soapbox. If you're done and if your story was engaging, they might walk out with you and ask you questions. Pray for outcome two.

   - The first story at the beginning of this chapter wasn't an elevator speech, although it was a story of faith. It took the speaker more than ten minutes to share it. It was a compelling tale, told in a friendly environment where participants were ready for training. The question would be, What are the key points that S could focus on to make the story into an elevator pitch? Take a moment to reread the story and find the key points. Write them down.

2. Backward and forward. You'll resist practicing. Ask God to help you! Most of your faith sharing is going to be most like the second story. You'll adapt your testimony to connect with what your person is telling you about their life. Know your own story backward and forward so that you can pull from it to insert it into a conversation that God is asking you to engage in. Practice is a big part of being able to do that.

   - If you're in the marketplace, you might already know about the need to practice your elevator pitch. A nurse/layperson in one of my seminars had moved into new-product and service development at the hospital where she worked. Her role was to introduce the service to doctors and nurses throughout the hospital. She knew exactly what I was talking about with the elevator pitch. She said practice, practice, practice was the key (and the way to Carnegie Hall).

   - Look again at the second story, and then at my testimony written out a few pages ahead. See if you can identify how I adapted my story to fit the conversation I was having. Write down your insights.

3. "I've always been a Christian." The third story reveals a common resistance among church people: that they don't have a story because they have always known Jesus. That's institutional thinking and for a lot of leaders, a place of guardedness. You have to do the work to get into the story, which means a lot of digging and reflection.

   - Instead, pursue your own narrative to see when you recognized the importance of being a Christ follower, even if it's just that you see your life with grace like Pastor N. Actually, not just . . .

   - Take a minute to pray and think about what has changed in your life because you follow Jesus. Write it down!

4. Cold-calling? That's not what this work is, but many Christ followers have a prejudice that it will be. It's the most prominent hurdle one faces when learning faith sharing. It's a misconception that you must hit someone over the head with the "truth." What is that, again? Most of us in the mainline tradition are far more moderate in our beliefs. That's why it's your experience of Jesus that matters most. You don't have to be a biblical scholar. You don't have to believe yours is the only way. You don't have to give anyone a pamphlet. Just be you, a friend, a person of faith. Be willing to tell that story to others when God prompts you.

   - But you won't know that God is prompting you without prayer. Enhance your prayer practices and other spiritual disciplines, such as fasting, study, solitude, and meditation. Increased spiritual practices are yet another hurdle for more institutional churches, leaders, and members. It's both a learning curve and a lifestyle change for most of us. Prayer will get you over the hump!

   - Return to the entry in chapter 1 about prayer disciplines. How is that going for you? Evaluate your progress in writing.

Backstory reflection questions

1. Say why what you just read was:

   - surprising,
   - engaging,
   - confusing,
   - encouraging, or
   - concerning.

2. Where did you see your church in what you read?

3. Where did you see yourself?

4. Who were you thinking about in what you just read?

5. What are you going to do next?

III. Rewriting the Story of Your Church's Future

Grow Comfortable With Faith-Talk

21. Learn from others' stories
22. The Fatih Story Alphabet
23. F.R.A.N.C.
24. Pursue outreach strategies
25. Pursue your story
26. Make videos

One week to one month

Another way to pursue this material

Chapter 4 (this chapter) could be a stand-alone chapter for some people in your church. If you want to follow that approach, you'll need to develop a few different groups to pursue this book study. Consider this approach:

- Group one: Teach this chapter—the faith sharing part (chapter 4)—to some members and make videos of those testimonies.
- Group two: Teach the deepening worship part (from the beginning of this book) to a different group—maybe musicians, worship designers, and liturgists. Include some of them in the group to whom you're teaching this chapter (chapter 4).
- Group three: Teach the following two chapters after this one to those who want to pursue faith development beyond church walls. This would be a new group comprising members of the other two groups.

The advantage of this approach is that you can engage several members with a portion of this book without involving everyone (since not everyone will want to do the entire thing). The disadvantage is that working through the material this way is more complex than any of the other options.

Churches with more than one hundred members may find that the complexity suits them because they have more resources, and they are accustomed to doing several things at once as a faith community, rather than focusing on one thing at a time. The caveat is not to jump over something or move fast without due diligence just because you're larger.

21. Learn from others' stories

My testimony

A long time ago, my husband and I were contemplating divorce. I was super confused about my marriage—and I had gotten involved in this institutional-type church, and God wasn't real to me there at all. One day on my way into the church building I thought, "I'm pretty screwed up. I should probably talk to somebody." I meant a counselor. Then I thought, "If I'm going to talk to someone, maybe it should be God." I meant that sarcastically. And then I thought, "Well if I'm going to talk to God, God must be real." I got this feeling of warmth that started at the top of my head and shot through my body, like I was being possessed by the Spirit of God. Not at all creepy. From there things in my life got worse before they got better, but they got better. God changed me and grew me up and grew my husband up, just as people. I am just so grateful for that, every single day.

A. Testimony Discussion Questions and Notes

a. How many words does this story have, and how long would it take to tell in conversation? Someone can read it aloud (with pauses and emphasis) and time it.

b. The use of the vernacular makes a story relatable to the person you're talking to. What are the vernacular words used in this story? Write down some words.

c. One's testimony should elicit questions or reactions from the engaged listener. What questions does this testimony elicit? Write those down.

B. S's Testimony

a. Reread S's testimony.

b. Now write out what you read in the first opening story as a first-person testimony following the guidelines you've already learned, above. We'll come back to what you wrote later in this chapter.

22. The Faith Story Alphabet

Backstory, **C**onflict, and **D**enouement (turning point). The "B-C-D" sequence is an easy way to remember what you must include in a faith story to make it compelling.

A. Breaking Down Testimonies with B-C-D

Where were B, C, and D, in:

a. my testimony?

b. S's testimony?

c. N's testimony?

B. Not the Alphabet but a Format

I have a client who is eager to learn this material but who speaks English as a second language. The language barrier often creates communication difficulties on both my side and his. He struggled with the faith story alphabet, so I devised this approach for his consideration. It follows the faith story alphabet without using that language.

a. What was the big, disruptive thing that happened to you?

b. Why did that happen?

c. When did you start praying and what was the result?

d. What did you learn about God?

Which approach suits your church best: B-C-D or the format?

23. F.R.A.N.C.

You don't have to make new friends to do outreach. You do have to rethink existing relationships to include faith talk. Doing so will challenge you. So make a F.R.A.N.C. list: Friends, Relatives, Acquaintances, Neighbors, Colleagues.

A. How to Make Your F.R.A.N.C. List

a. Sit a moment in silence and prepare to pray.

b. Ask that God will allow you to hear the names of people you could reach out to

c. After the prayer, write down as many names in each category of F.R.A.N.C. as you can think of that you're in connection with.

d. Pray again. Ask God to show you who on the list needs the most faith talk.

e. Circle one name in each category.

f. Pray again. Ask God to help you select one name from among the five you circled.

g. Star one name. That's where you'll start.

h. Take on 1-1. Pray for the one person you are focusing on right now for about one minute. See below.

A Note to Leaders

Most laypeople can pray for only one person at a time. Encourage them in this direction. When you read about the numbers in the next chapter, you'll see that it will work with members praying for only one person. That's because, as the project leader, you will be reaching out to multiple people and praying for them.

- Make your F.R.A.N.C. list
- Prayerfully identify the person to pray for
- Schedule your 1-1-1-1 prayer

24. Pursue outreach strategies

Outreach involves ethics, which are like strategies to help you move forward in growing comfortable with faith sharing, including the strategy of:

A. The 1-1-1-1- Prayer
   Memorize this prayer or create one of your own:
   God, please open the doorway to conversations about faith today
   Now repeat that prayer according to the following strategy: Pray for one minute

   a. For one person on your F.R.A.N.C. list

   b. On one day of the week

   c. At 1 p.m.

B. You Becoming You
   When you pursue prayer for someone else, God shapes you into who you are and who God intended you to be. Your prayers for 1-1-1-1 include: mission, trust, skill development, and etiquette.

   a. Mission
      Take on faith sharing as a disciple because God has called you to it. God matures you in faith when you do.

   b. Trust
      God is the one who produces the results of your prayers and your activities in the mission field. That grows you as a person of faith.

   c. Skill development: If you played football, you needed to know the plays. If you were a golfer, you'd be constantly working on your swing (and your putting). When you go down the road of learning to be you, you must prepare with the same earnestness and intensity for muscle memory.

   d. Etiquette: You won't inject faith talk into a conversation with an existing friend without asking if it's okay to do it. You ask God and your person. Then:

      i. God taps you on the shoulder and says, "You should tell your friend about me."

      ii. You say to your friend, I am resonating with what you're saying, and if it's okay, I'd love to share from my own heart, and it's going to be about God. Would that be okay?

      iii. Your friend says no. That's not a problem unless you make it one. That grows you.

      iv. Your friend says yes. You hear yourself, and it grows you in faith.

C. The Personal Outreach Plan
   Make a list of the things you already do with the person you're praying for on F.R.A.N.C. If you don't do anything with that person, make a list of what you could do. When you pray 1-1-1-1, include prayers for getting together with your friend.

D. Introversion
   Introverts do well in one-to-one chats. Most conversations about faith with people outside of church walls are one-on-one. Extroverts can learn from introverts in developing faith-sharing chops.

Answer the following questions:

- Are you an extrovert or an introvert?
- What is your fear level about reaching out?
- How can prayer help you reach out?
- What did you learn from F.R.A.N.C. and various outreach strategies?
- What will you do next?

25. Pursue your story

The writing of your testimony is a great thing to do in a group because you'll get immediate feedback. If you're going through this material on your own, pursue the activity of trying out your testimony on close friends and family. Ask for honest feedback. Don't be flattered if they don't give you any.

Following a Sequence for Writing Your Testimony

1. Pray
    - Discernment on which part of your life with Jesus to write about for your testimony
    - Hearing God in the silence
2. Write
    - What's B-C-D for your story? Make a bulleted list.
    - Put the bulleted list in story form using fewer than two hundred words.
    - Use vernacular and otherwise common language.
3. Share (for feedback)
    - Follow the leader's guide for pursuing input in a group or on your own.

Test and Hone

- Ask a friend, acquaintance, or relative for some time. Tell them you want them to be a guinea pig for hearing your testimony. You'll need at least fifteen minutes.
- Ask questions about what they heard.
- Ask if they had any questions from what they heard.
- Pray that God will use you and your story.

Adapt Your Testimony

Below are two scenarios. Both happened to me but I'm not writing them with me featured in the stories. Instead, I gave my role to S, and then to N. These examples show you how to adapt a testimony in the moment.

A. Scene One: Three women

The three young women were lingering around the dinner table at (S's) (Pastor N's) house, after everyone else had stepped away to chat in other parts of the house. The women had started talking about abortion. One friend confessed that she'd had one. The other friend was upset when she heard that because she had lost a child, stillborn, while unmarried, although she had gotten married since then and not to the stillborn baby's father. (S) (N) was very moved by what she heard. She said,

S's possible response:

"As long as we're putting things out there, I once almost took my own life. But then I heard this voice telling me I was good and loved. I figured it was God talking to me. So I didn't do it. I was messed up, but it took me a while to get past those dark thoughts. So I know that no one can judge you, and that God doesn't judge you."

N's possible response:

"You know, I'm totally moved by you guys being so real with each other. I had a friend growing up whose mom was sick and institutionalized while growing up. I felt lost for my friend. Over the years, I prayed for my friend and her mom and had some conversations with my friend as we got older about her resentment toward her mom. She had a hard time forgiving her mom, but I think she did, ultimately. Do you guys carry any guilt? I don't think you need to, if you do . . ."

Answer the following questions:

- What parts of S's and N's stories did they share, and what parts did they leave out?
- Do you think either one could have shared anything different? What?
- After you speak to someone spiritually in a way that reveals something about you, the person often will have questions. What questions would you have if you had been one of the women who shared, and S or N responded in this way?

B. Scene Two: Retail

The customer's husband was waiting for his wife while (S) (N), the sales associate, was running clothes back and forth to her. The husband had engaged (S) (N) in conversation and somehow it wound around to the church. (S) (N) asked him if he had grown up in the church. He had, but he had left it because the church was so institutional. (S) (N) agreed.

S's possible response:

"Yeah," she said, "I was divorced, and my parents didn't condone it for religious reasons, which put a wedge between us. That was tough because the divorce put me behind financially, and I could have used help. And that's right about the time I literally heard God's voice telling to rein it in and feel better about myself."

N's possible response:

Yes, churches get super institutional. Everything is like a program. I've been a lifelong Christian and the one thing I know I do well is pray and see life from God's eyes. That's not a program at all, do you think?

Answer the following questions:

- What parts of S's and N's stories did they share and what parts did they leave out?
- Do you think either one could have shared anything different? What?
- What questions might you have had for S or N if you had been the retail customer?

C. Scene Three: You're the lead

Substitute your name for S or N in the two sample stories above.

- How are you feeling about your testimony?
- What responses do you expect from your friends?

26. Make videos

You have room in worship for a testimonial video every week if you have the capacity to create one. Someone in your church is probably technical and can help you take this on. Consider the following input from a videographer on video development.

A. What's a Testimonial Video?

A testimonial video is a recording of someone sharing their testimony. Or it's a recording of someone talking about how they got connected with your church, or how Jesus is becoming real to them, or maybe even about the doubts they have. All of those are different types of testimonies.

B. Why Are Testimonial Videos Influential?

Testimonial videos are incredibly influential for persons in seats. The medium itself is influential (video). As well, peers influence peers. When you see your friend in a video talking about their faith journey, your heart opens.

C. How Do You Put a Testimonial Video Together?

Some larger churches have full-time paid videographers who develop testimonial videos from among members and new participants. Smaller churches can do videos too, with their phones. A member who has written a short testimony can record it as a selfie. Or, you can do an interview. Follow these steps:

1. Setup
   - Select a good recording platform.
   - Pursue tutorials online for video editing.
2. Recording and editing
   - Develop a repeatable intro and outro.
     - Intro: how each video begins
     - Outro: how each one ends

- Be in touch with the talent (the one featured in the video) or subject a few weeks before recording.
- Provide questions that you're going to ask.
- Put questions in a sequence to facilitate editing.
    - Questions could be: Did you prepare a one-minute testimony? What was the process like? Can you share your testimony? Why did you decide to be part of this outreach process? How have you changed?
    - Plan for four hours to record and edit a single one-minute video.

Caveat: Don't put a smartphone on a stand and ask people to stand in front and share their story. They won't know what to do!

- Instead, schedule the recording and plan to edit one testimonial video to see how it goes. Test-market it among truth-tellers to see how it comes off. Improve it so that you can show it in worship.
- It must be one minute long or less!
- For high impact, tie the testimony to a message!

Rewriting Your Story Reflection Questions

1. Say why what you just read was:
    - surprising,
    - engaging,
    - confusing,
    - encouraging, or
    - concerning.
2. Where did you see your church in what you read?
3. Where did you see yourself?
4. Who were you thinking about in what you just read?

5. Additional chapter questions:
    - What is your biggest stumbling block with this chapter and with faith sharing?
    - What could you do to get over the hurdle of teaching people faith sharing?
    - Are you, the leader, doing this work yourself to see what you can learn about it? How can you incorporate this lifestyle change into the way you lead every day of your life?
6. What are you going to do next?

Chapter postscript: Not ready for prime time . . .

Even after all the work on developing your and other members' testimonies, you'll find that some members you've trained don't want to put themselves out there to share it beyond church walls. No worries. You can help them come into faith sharing through the back door with the outline on the next page titled "Community Interview Conversation Recorder." To use this resource, do the following:

- Study F.R.A.N.C. Ask the member to pray over their F.R.A.N.C. list and come up with one person on the list to call.
- Develop the ask. The member will call to ask the friend about their church life and interests; no need to couch the ask. You need to get comfortable with the ask.
- Develop the questions. It's important that you have questions that seem to matter in your context. Don't just take my suggestions! Use these ideas to trigger questions of your own. Provide a list of questions for the person calling their friend, and have them go down the list, asking questions and writing down answers. Questions could include:
- Why did you stop going to church? (Why don't you go, why do you go, etc)
- What do you love about your faith community?
- What should the church be talking about that you never hear them talk about?
- What shouldn't the church be talking about?
- If you were going to design a worship service, what would be in it? What kind of music, how much music, what other things, etc.
- What questions do you have about God?
- Who else do you know that hyou think would be a good person for me to talk with about church life? Can you make the connection between them and me?
- Make the call. Schedule it, then do it. It can be a video chat or a live and in-person meeting.
- Fill in the form and return it to discuss—one-on-one with the project leader or in a group of individuals working on the same task.
- Do it again? Maybe yes, maybe not?
- Compile the info. This can be an excellent resource for determining who in your area to reach out to. We'll talk about that in chapter 6.

Community Interviews Conversation Recorder / Date ____________________

My name ____________________

Name of person ____________________ New before now ____________________

Where we interacted ____________________

Key questions and responses

Q.____________________

A.____________________

A.____________________

Q.____________________

A.____________________

A.____________________

Q.____________________

A.____________________

A.____________________

Q.____________________

A.____________________

A.____________________

Q.____________________

A.____________________

A.____________________

Q.____________________

A.____________________

A.____________________

Gave them my card / info __________ Willing to be contacted again __________

Their info ____________________

Chapter Five

DOING THE MATH

Chapter Notes

The most offensive chapter follows the most practical one. That's no accident. You won't sustain anything you do with the first four chapters without a serious look at your numbers—where they are now and where they need to be if you are going to extend your church's footprint into the neighborhood. You must pursue numbers to build a system of faith sharing that can move a congregation from an inwardly focused to an outwardly focused one. That can seem inauthentic to some church people. In fact, numbers are the opposite if you don't over-blow them. When you grasp how many people need to know your church exists for your church to do ministry effectively, you can no longer fool yourself into thinking that you're declining for any other reason than not sharing faith. Let this chapter adjust your thinking. Though it may seem daunting at first, you can accomplish everything this chapter introduces to you numerically, even if it's demanding.

Chapter Notes reflection question

What is your expectation of this chapter?

I. Real-Life Coaching Stories

The Cringe Factor

Even in a culture in which new people don't just automatically show up on a church's doorstep, churches do get what some refer to as "drop-ins." No one personally invited them; they appear. A twenty-first-century drop-in is probably not someone who is without a church background. Maybe they moved and need a new church. Maybe they had a falling out with their church and left, and now they want to find a new faith community. Whatever the case, a few new Christians in your area will church-hop or shop. If you do get a drop-in, they'll probably want to know if they can fit in. Fitting in could mean seeing enough people there so they can be assured there is some life in the faith community. The new person that's looking for a healthy, missional church might not even enter the church if the parking lot doesn't have enough cars in it. They know that if they walk in, everyone will turn to stare because a new person is such an anomaly. That's known as the cringe factor. These people want to turn and run!

Most new people will come to the church because of their relationship with you, especially those without a significant church background. But even your personal connections might know enough to drive by on a Sunday morning to see if the cars in the parking lot look like theirs and their friends' cars. They'll notice if there are enough cars, with enough people in seats, to avoid the cringe factor. The cringe factor is already at work on the drive-by.

Capture Rate

I had one client who strongly opposed intentional outreach, claiming it was inauthentic. This client held some large-scale events at the church campus. You might think that sounds like outreach, but it's not, exactly. It's a passive approach when you don't staff the event with members who are trained to engage people in conversation and share their faith.

The church gave away items at the events to capture guests' names and contact information. Bad idea, I told them. If the church is after authenticity, then it is shooting itself in the foot. A person who likely distrusts the church is now suddenly on the church's mailing list after the church told them they were taking names and contact information for a giveaway.

This church thought they'd get at least some people to come to worship from the thousands that participated in their various events over a couple of years. They got only a few. That's a very low capture rate. Why would anyone attend a church that engages in bait-and-switch tactics? The church gained visibility in the neighborhood, which is a great reason to host large-scale events. However, visibility doesn't attract many new people to worship without a personal connection.

Deep down, I don't think the leaders really believed the number of names they added to their mailing list would yield an influx of new people. Deep down, I'm pretty sure they knew the capture rate would be low because they've been on the receiving end of such mailing lists they didn't sign up for. What the leaders believed instead was that by putting together a mailing list without asking people if they wanted to be on it, they wouldn't have to challenge their biases about outreach. That part worked for them.

This is a typical example that shows that even those who resist paying attention to numbers still pay attention to numbers, just not in a way that would benefit them or the new people in the long run. If you do the work to increase the capture rate, you won't get nearly as many names for your mailing list. But you'll get more than if you pursue names mechanically, since almost everyone who didn't agree to be on it will quickly opt out of the list.

Coaching stories reflection questions:

What points did the stories raise?

Did any describe you or your church? How?

II. Backstories of Institutionalism (and some formulas)

Insights into the opening stories

I've found that most church people respond to the discussion about numerical growth in one of two ways. One is with disdain: "We don't want to be a megachurch." The other is with arrogance, "WE'RE a MEGAchurch!" We all know stories of megachurches and leaders that have fallen from grace. Maybe we saw it coming because of the arrogance. On the other hand, the church that's concerned about too much growth is, well, in denial. Using numbers helps you see reality. Numbers tell a story. And this is a story book. Those who repeat that they don't want to be a megachurch are subtly suggesting that numbers aren't significant. In fact, they're critical. When you embrace them, they'll rewrite the ending of your church's story—if you don't make it all about the numbers. Growth is, and always will be, about sharing faith.

Critical mass

To sustain your service over time, get to critical mass. Declining churches lack critical mass. To achieve it, understand it. Critical mass comprises several key components.

A. Critical Mass and Room Size

Room size, as in relation to the number of people in the room, is part of understanding critical mass. A church needs enough people in one room at one time to sustain a worship gathering so that new people don't feel exposed when they walk in. In the chapter on worship development, we discussed critical mass without explicitly referring to it. We called it "size dynamics." The story in chapter 2, titled "Mainline Church," also provides a picture of critical mass without explicitly naming it.

In the mainline church, the room sat about sixty people. It felt packed with about fifty in attendance at roughly 80 percent full. However, they could rearrange the seating so that thirty-five people would be comfortable in the room at about 60 percent capacity. They rarely went lower, but they didn't pack out the place every week either. When they did, they had a small café where you could watch the service on the numerous screens in the room.

If your worship meeting space is less than 60 percent full, it becomes challenging to accommodate new people because the available space is disproportionately small relative to the number of attendees. You don't have critical mass. Therefore, you need to shrink your space to add new people and achieve critical mass.

B. Critical Mass and Social Momentum

As crucial as room size is for understanding critical mass, it's just scratching the surface of what critical mass is. Understanding the deeper side of critical mass will help you reach it. My coach used to refer to critical mass as "social momentum." Here's an illustration:

My husband and I traveled to a mountainous, rural area to visit a friend. While driving through the rolling countryside we stumbled upon a restaurant on a Saturday afternoon at about 1 p.m. that served BBQ and pie. And we were hungry! The restaurant was overlooking an expansive gully. It seemed promising. There were a few large, nice-looking pickups in the parking lot, and there were a couple of beaters. Not many vehicles, but then it was lunchtime in a not heavily populated area. As we slowed down to consider if we should stop, up came a pack of (motor) bikers—maybe about ten. They pulled into the lot, got off their bikes, removed their helmets, and exposed their bandanas and beards. They walked in. So we parked and followed their lead. Good decision! I still remember the outstanding short ribs we ate, and the cherry pie for dessert. And I remember the view. Spectacular. I remember the bikers and their bikes in an indelible image in my head. Fun! My husband and I both remember the experience positively, although neither of us remembers the name of the restaurant. But if you went to the Arkansas Grand Canyon and asked around, I'll bet the locals would know the place I'm referring to. Enjoy your meal!

Social momentum for the church is the requirement that the church engage with and pursue the secular culture so that its mission field takes their message of hope in Jesus seriously. Without social influence, the local church languishes. My coach used to say, "If the locals don't connect with your church, no one will." To communicate with the locals, value their daily lives.

Local expectations

The church grows from Jerusalem to Judea to Samaria to the ends of the earth. Jerusalem is where the locals live. Part of what you're doing when you're pursuing critical mass is mentally and practically drawing the boundaries of Jerusalem.  Find an entry on using demographic studies to draw the boundaries of Jerusalem in part II, phase 2, entry 4. The next entry, #5, will be worth your read too.

Effective outreach begins in your backyard, where the locals have expectations of what life is going to be like. One of those expectations is the size of public, or social, gatherings. Style goes along with that expectation. So if there are enough cars in front of your building during worship time that remind an observer of other social gatherings he or she participates in locally, and if they recognize and relate to the style of the vehicles, then the observer knows something of value is going on in your church. They can imagine themselves and their friends being part of your faith community because your public view helps your observer grow more comfortable with their own participation there. They expect others like them to be inside should they decide to come see you during worship because someone invited them or because your church has gathered a positive reputation in town. They don't worry so much that they'll stick out like a sore thumb. That would keep them away.

But hang on a minute. It's not quite that simple. You might think that because the restaurant with the bikers had about twenty people in it, I'm saying that your worship gathering should be at about twenty also. That's not what I'm saying. Your worship service could be a small venue, based on the restaurant experience. You have to be sure, though, that this place is not an anomaly in town. And then, you have to frame what a small venue is for worship. Tricky.

Minimum worship numbers

Is there a minimum number for a worship gathering to make it "public"? Some might disagree with me, but I say yes. Many churches have worship gatherings with fewer than twenty. That's like a big small group. It's very, very difficult for a new person to fit into an established setting like that, where the same people come weekly and everyone knows everyone else and all their life issues. If you're going to have a worship gathering in which people stand up, sit down, sing, and participate en masse, the new person is going to feel exposed. There has to be a minimum number of people in the worship gathering for group dynamics to improve for newcomers if your church is going to reach new people. I say that number is about fifty. That's when you see fewer individual faces and more of a collective body.

For fifty to feel right in worship, your space has to seat about one hundred max. Or if your space might seat about seventy-five max, perhaps you could get away with forty, or at the very least, thirty-five. I've seen and coached small-venue gatherings that are modern, with spaces that aren't cavernous and way too big for the gathering. Sometimes a church like this will have multiple gatherings at the same size. Now you have a large church comprising three or four gatherings of thirty-five to fifty people every week. By aiming for fifty, you could get a few less. But you also could get more. By aiming for twenty, you could get a few less, but it's unlikely you'll get more.

Number, style, and being who you are

The leader's role is to discern critical mass for your worship service by understanding the behavior and values of the locals in social gatherings. You'll have a "hard" or concrete number to pray for. No one can tell you precisely what the number will be. You have to figure it out. It might take you a few days of driving around in your area to see what the parking lots of local establishments look like during prime time. That includes other churches that are bigger than yours. You'll look for the number and the style of the vehicles.

If a church parking lot has a lot of high-end and expensive vehicles, you'll know that the church won't have many poorer people in attendance, if any. I've coached a couple of churches that had to rethink how to reach people below the poverty line in their area because of their members' wealth. It wasn't through public worship, much to their chagrin. But that's not their fault. It's no one's fault. The poorer people they reached out to couldn't get past the style of cars in the parking lot to begin to feel that they'd fit in should they come in, even though they were invited.

Most churches will find that social momentum is to some degree homogeneous. The diversity they seek comes from members pursuing friends and others they already know. They have affinity, but not uniformity.

Social momentum and trust, not attraction

But with all the discussion about seeing critical mass from the outside, literally, you may be tempted to confuse social momentum with attraction. The institutional church tries to attract new people to its worship services rather than to develop personal connections between the church and the neighborhood through faith development. New people aren't going to come to your church just because you look relevant from the outside.

So don't go renting a bunch of cars or members to try to show off. Don't try to make everyone think you've got it all together from the outside so that they come into your church when they drive by. They're still not going to do that, for the most part—not without a personal relationship with someone. If they do set foot inside, they'd know you're not telling the truth if you try to fake it from the outside. You believe it's attraction that brings them, and it's not.

It's the pursuit of God that brings them. Reaching new people remains always about the content of your message. Even if someone does feel they can learn from you by what they see on the outside, they won't stick around if they don't learn from you.

Critical mass builds trust, and trust is the heartbeat of social momentum. When you do not yet have critical mass and you're trying to get to it, you are not going to be able to connect with a lot of people. But you will be able to connect with a few. And then you'll connect with a few more and a few more, as you build connections in the mission field on your way to a number that allows you to connect with even more people.

Room size and critical mass redux

For those new people you reach out to when you're not yet at critical mass for your worship service, the room size will help or hurt you. If you're in a room that's far too big for your current membership and worship participation, then it's an indication that you're languishing. You haven't downsized for one reason or another. The downsizing shows that you're willing to deal with the hard stuff. That's the pushback from members and staff who don't want to change. Languishing is the opposite of social momentum. You're not giving yourself a chance to build community, which is very difficult to develop in a room that's far too big for your numbers. You have no social momentum. You have discouragement.

C. Critical Mass and launching

If you are starting a new worship service and you have but a handful of people right now, or if your church has declined and you have but a handful or two of people left, the process is the same to achieve critical mass. You develop faith-sharing chops. Then you bring your heart with you to talk about faith with the mission field beyond church walls. You follow the church planting process to get to the number you've discerned is the minimum number for your context for worship to thrive. Then you launch. The church-planting process of launching is a tried-and-true approach to building your numbers so that you can reach critical mass. You would use the same approach whether you're starting a church, launching a new worship service, or revitalizing an existing one. The launch process enables you to build social momentum by directly targeting your key metrics, which is based in percentages.

D. Critical Mass and Percentages

In a helpful episode of *The Carey Nieuwhof Leadership Podcast*, we learn about how churches grow in new starts, including how they reach critical mass.[1] Starting a new service or transforming an existing one is almost exactly like planting a church; applying the church-planting numbers to rebuilding in-person worship is a valuable exercise. Let's consider three categories of people who will come your way through our outreach efforts: transfers, de-churched, and never churched.

1. Transfers

In this Carey Nieuwhof podcast episode, "The New Math of Church Plants," you learn that when you start a church, you'll get about 40 percent transfers—the highest of three sets of numbers that represent the people who will populate your new start.[2] In another helpful podcast, *The Great De-churching*, we hear that the number one reason people leave a church is that they've moved.[3] When I attended church planter training in about 2000, one of the key teachings was how to leverage local information about new residents. The research shared in the podcast reinforces that teaching. In other words, don't think you're sheep-stealing when you reach out to new people who are looking for a new church. Transfers provide a boost to the church-planting process of reaching critical mass for churches starting or revamping worship services within their congregations. I didn't know the stats before listening to the podcast. But it rang true because I've seen it in various new starts.

2. De-churched

The next category for populating your new worship project is 20 percent de-churched persons. In researching *The Great De-churching,* author Jim Davis states that they determined that online-only participants are de-churched.[4] They don't participate in worship in the building. It's common to hear complaints from church leaders of all sizes about how difficult it is to get online-only attendees into the building and into the worship gathering. My own perspective is that most churches believe they have a lot more online members than they actually do. That's step one for a reality check. Step two is finding ways to connect with those who online. If you understand that new people won't randomly show up, you'll see the need to build relationships, even with those who are online, and give them a reason to visit the building. That reason will extend beyond just a good worship service. It will have something to do with pursuing their identity as Christ followers by following Jesus into the mission field. It also has something to do with the dynamics of the public experience of meeting God in person in community and communicating that to new people. Revisit chapter 2 for understanding.

3. Never-churched

The final category of "The New Math of Church Plants" is 5–10 percent of your total new-start numbers who are truly unchurched, never churched, or who have never had a relationship with Jesus.[5] If your church is pursuing outreach through faith sharing, you're likely to encounter people in this category. It's a low percentage, but it will happen. Thus, it's an important category to prepare to meet. I see this category driving the other two, because you'll have to be ready to help a person in this category take an overt step toward Jesus. That's about the "max" that you'll go in faith sharing. All other aspects of faith sharing and outreach are demanding to a lesser degree. In the next chapter, we'll pursue how you help someone who has never embraced Jesus or the church take an intentional step toward faith.

E. Critical Mass, The Capture Rate, and Starting Your Launch Team

"The New Math of Church Plants" (podcast) also offers insights into the numerical benchmarks for launching a church.[6] This is where the second opening story in this chapter comes in. That story is about the capture rate. That's common language for sales, which, when applied to the church, can seem unchristian. It's a helpful image, though, because it shows you that, in fact, you do have to be intentional about adding new people to your midst. They're not going to come to you automatically. As told in the capture rate opening story, you can be authentic about engaging new people, or you can be inauthentic. We endeavor for all outreach strategies to reveal the main purpose behind this work: sharing Jesus. Intentionality is not automatically inauthentic.

For starting or transforming worship in your church, you'll need to capture about ⅓ of critical mass by launch, and then you'll triple your numbers at or through the launch. That means that if you're starting your new project out of an existing church with members, the size of your initial group is going to be about 10 percent to 12 percent of your critical mass number that you've discerned is local.

If you want to continue, then move on to the task portion of this chapter. You'll learn some growth formulas, starting with assembling your launch team.

Backstory reflection questions

1. Say why what you just read was:
    - o surprising,
    - o engaging,
    - o confusing,
    - o encouraging, or
    - o concerning.
2. Where did you see your church in what you read?
3. Where did you see yourself?
4. Who were you thinking about in what you just read?
5. What are you going to do next?

III. Rewriting the Story of Your Church's Future

If you're an individual Christ follower pursuing this material to grow as a disciple who makes disciples, you don't need a system. Just work your way through the workbook and put prayer and your testimony to work.

If you're a church leader trying to impact in-person worship through faith sharing, you need a system. The system you build to bring people along to change your culture has a prominent numerical component. Most of what you'll do in part II of this workbook is numerically based. Note the suggested timeline at the bottom of the step-up column. That represents what it will take you to absorb the content of this chapter, not necessarily do much with it beyond that.

Accessing the numbers in this chapter is your starting point for considering how they'll impact your church specifically. You'll have more to do in part II to further clarify your capture rate.

Doing Math

27. Critical mass for your service
28. Launch team numbers
29. Contacts and connections
30. Organizing a digital faith community

One week to one month

27. Critical mass for your service

The project leader's task in a worship transformation project is to determine the critical mass for their worship project. Get a group together to go through your town to see what the various venues are like when they're serving lunches, dinners, happy hour, or coffee. Or when the gym is really crowded—how crowded is crowded? Look at hospital parking lots during visiting hours. Drive by local high school football games. Drive past other growing churches during prime worship time. What do you see? As you drive, consider these concepts:

Mainline church

The church featured in chapter 2, known as mainline church, was in a college town. The university is very well known as a football powerhouse, so it's common for massive numbers of people to swarm the city all at once (for sporting events). But everywhere you go in the town, there are small venues—like small coffee shops or restaurants. The church seated about sixty when packed, but it was rarely filled. They had multiple services at a smaller venue, the right size for the group. They were a large church comprising several small venues.

Fun church and big church

The other two churches featured in chapter 2 were in the suburbs. Drive by hospital parking lots in the suburbs. They're always packed. Not so in a rural area. Suburban restaurants are often chains and seat perhaps in the hundreds at capacity. It's challenging to justify holding a worship gathering in the suburbs that draws fewer than one hundred people, since suburbanites are accustomed to being around others.

Numerical formulas scale. If your church has twenty members and you find that the critical mass is thirty to fifty, apply the numerical formulas to grow by ten to thirty new people to sustain the service. You can grow from twenty to fifty and from fifty to one hunded by launching and relaunching.

Gather a group to conduct prayer walks in your area to discern a critical mass for your specific worship project. Follow some of the guidelines in this entry for discerning what is local. What's the culture of your area? How does that impact the numbers you need for critical mass in your service? Schedule a date to explore your neighborhood. Process the results as a group. Write down the number for the critical mass for your service.

Anecdotal

My husband and I recently moved to the next town south of our previous home. We know the area, but not that well. We went for coffee one Saturday morning in the local downtown. It's a quirky area, with small-venue restaurants, a fairly good-sized sports bar, and one local, personal, creative, unique, and very crowded coffee shop. We couldn't sit down. If that were my only source of information, I might conclude that a new worship gathering would be small-venue. However, this town consistently has one of the highest two-person income rankings in the state of Minnesota. It's very educated and wealthy. If you follow Ryan Burge, you know that education is an indicator of religious pursuit. Educated people are more likely to be churchgoers. And one of the most well-known megachurches around is in this town. I used to be on staff there as the director of church planting. The church I started is also in this same town, and that's a thriving, midsized congregation. The gym I go to is close to my home. It's huge and pretty upscale. I go there because they have the best pools and I love to swim. This town used to be rural, so there remains some niche identity. But there is a ton of housing here now, with massive growth. With all of that in mind, I'm not sure a small-venue service is going to take root in a small-venue church in spite of a few indicators to the contrary. Maybe. If the megachurch wanted to do something small venue, I think it would work. But if I were starting a new service in this town out of a smaller congregation or as a new church, I think I'd lean toward a minimum of one hundred to reach critical mass.

28. Launch Team Numbers

A launch team is a group that works with the leader to launch or relaunch a new or existing service, transforming it. The launch team adds new people throughout the launch process, then disbands after the launch. Pursue the following formula to assemble the right-sized group that achieves critical mass for your service in your local context. For critical mass of one hundred:

- Gather 10–12 percent of critical mass with members (ten to twelve persons);
- get to 3 × ten persons by the time of launch, with new people (30 to 40 people);
- expect about twelve to sixteen new people from other churches, about six to eight returning to the church after an absence, and about one or two unchurched;
- triple the number of new people you've gathered by launch with the launch itself (90 to 120 people total);
- expect about thirty-six to forty-eight to be transfers, about eighteen to twenty-four to be dechurched, and about two to four to be never churched; and
- meet in a room that seats roughly 30–40 percent more than 90–120, or approximately 130-ish, give or take.

29. Contacts and Connections

When growing your launch team, you'll make contacts and connections. This entry is devoted to helping readers understand the difference between the two concepts and their yin-yang relationship. If used correctly, making contacts and connections enables you to reach critical mass.
The following calculations assume achieving a critical mass of one hundred in worship.

A. Definitions

- Contacts: people who provide you with contact information—interested in your church.
- Connections: exposed to what you're doing but won't provide personal information.

B. Make enough connections to support contacts.

- Make twenty thousand connections (not a typo) to reach one thousand contacts, with one hundred engaging in worship each week.
    - You need approximately twenty times as many names in your contact list as will attend your church weekly, since less than 20 percent attend weekly.
    - In other words, you need approximately two thousand names on your contact list to have about one hundred people in worship weekly.
- Since it takes about ten invites for one person to agree to participate in your church, your connections should be about twenty thousand. Many people need to know that your church exists for it to grow numerically.
- Your launch team will make most of the contacts individually. That includes the project leader, who will make multiple individual contacts beyond any single member of the launch team.

- You will create buzz beyond individual contacts through various launching activities, from developing your launch team to the launch itself (or reaching critical mass).
- You won't count the connections. You'll feel them.

Consider your current worship attendance. Now consider how many connections you have in the community in which you live. Do you think it's in the thousands range? If not, you have a good idea of why you have declined.

Do you have an idea of what critical mass is for your worship gathering? What size launch team is needed to produce critical mass? Who will be on your launch team? This list is currently tentative, but it's worth praying over now. You'll develop your launch team not long before or even as you start part II of this workbook.

30. Organizing a Digital Faith Community

Consider developing an online faith community to keep the conversation about numbers going, as well as to pursue learning faith sharing from one another (participants in the digital community). Your digital faith community won't replace in-person worship. It's a group. You'll learn about groups in part II, phase 3. The initial purpose of this group is to provide a place for members and their guests to gather who need more time to discern whether to pursue the church or stay connected as they explore faith sharing. You can teach about faith sharing in this community. You can also invite your guests to it, and they'll be part of the burgeoning identity of your church as a church of disciples who make disciples ("the faith-sharing church"). You may not actually establish this faith community right now. But this would be a good time to consider how you'll organize it and why. Ideally, this group will have taken root by the time you become involved in outreach beyond church walls. It will take organization and leadership to develop and sustain it, just as with in-person worship.

1. Purpose (three reasons to develop an online faith community)

- Ongoing training. You won't get to everything you want to get to through a book study. You'll need more connections to impart wisdom and establishing an online community helps you get those.
- Encouragement. The online faith community is 24-7 and, therefore, a place of constant interaction. Online prayer will be a significant area of support for outreach beyond church walls.
- Numerical growth. You'll find that there are people "out there" who want an online experience before they want an in-person one. Adding new people to your online faith community is part of the numerical strategy that takes time to build.

2. Process (the challenges to developing an online faith community)

The online faith community is an excellent tool for outreach and worship. It's also new territory and thus difficult. The difficulty is twofold.

a. Technical.

- Platform. Google "Discord for religious online discussion groups" or "FB/Meta for religious online discussion groups."

- Agreeing to the platform. Not all your people and followers will already be using the platform you selected. That's as it should be since this approach is invitational, not attractional. However, some members and invitees won't want to engage with a specific platform. That's okay, but you might not think so right away.
- Learning curve. Using any platform will create a learning curve that someone will have to navigate.
- Cost. Generally, the use of social media platforms should be unrestricted.

b. Organizational.

- Participation. It's a slow start to getting your online faith community up and running. Someone is going to have to keep promoting it, and that can seem like a waste of time when one leader is so busy with all the work associated with gathering new people.
- Value. You'll need to recognize the importance of this group to keep it going when it seems to be progressing slowly. You may need to find a leader for it that's not the leader of the faith-sharing process outside of church walls.
- Technical overseer/s: A good position to develop would be someone who keeps studying the platform and can help you use it even if they're not the primary communicator on that platform.
- Host/s: Hosts lead prayer or post according to a posting plan and strategy. Developing this position (volunteer mostly) will help you get some legs.

Rewriting your story reflection questions

1. Say why what you just read was:
    - surprising,
    - engaging,
    - confusing,
    - encouraging, or
    - concerning.
2. Where did you see your church in what you read?
3. Where did you see yourself?
4. Who were you thinking about in what you just read?

- Additional chapter questions:
- What math formulas made the most sense to you?

5. What math formulas can you apply to your church right now?

6. What are you going to do next?

Chapter Postscript: Belief

There is not a single church or church leader who takes on worship development through faith sharing without experiencing some level of panic along the way. It's normal to feel panicked after reading this chapter. The key to overcoming panic is to remember what God has called you to do. You are pursuing faith development beyond church walls as the primary way of following God through worship. Then you are rebuilding in-person worship through your journey. God is not going to abandon you. It may seem that way when you are struggling with any one of the many parts of this process. However, God has prepared people who want to connect with you and your church. Belief is a mighty antidote to taking the plunge toward both numerical and spiritual growth. Keep praying.

Chapter Six

COUNTERING CULTURE

You the leader (pastor, staff, lay, paid, non-paid, volunteer)

Learns about worship beyond church walls by following God to create community not just get more people to quickly fix in-person worship

Trusting God for all outcomes on the journey even loss, even when facing angry emotions in self and others that might get bigger when you face them, not smaller

While learning faith talk and your own story to share it so you can just be you, always a Christ follower

And discerning next steps for the church because of some of the numbers

To pursue the secular culture to remain countercultural as a value of in-person worship

Chapter Notes

The final piece of groundwork you'll produce in part I is now, in this chapter. It's also a transition point: If you complete the tasks, you'll be better prepared for part II. Knowing who you are as a faith community is key to leaving the church building and engaging in mission work with those who are far from God and the church. When you know who you are, you can interact in the mission field with much more purpose and fruit because your boundaries will be defined by your heart, not judgement. You'll use the culture to remain countercultural. This chapter pushes you to be clear. The clarity will be your identity: Who are you, and what do you want people to know about Jesus and the church? Keep asking and answering that question through this chapter.

Chapter Notes reflection question

What is your expectation of this chapter?

I. Real-Life Coaching Stories

Pushing the Boundaries

I live in the greater metropolitan area of Minneapolis-St. Paul. A well-known church in this area has garnered considerable attention over the years for its Christmas activities. That's when they give away cars or televisions or big vacations to get people in the door so that the new people can hear the gospel message. Would you and your church do something like that? Don't be too quick to answer.

Self-imposed Boundaries

I coached a pastor in a multicultural area who was Caucasian, and her spouse was African American. Their children were biracial. The church had a community-giveaway ministry that drew a large crowd, but none of those people attended the church's worship gatherings. The big question was always how to bridge the gap between the social justice ministry and the worship gathering. The answer was intentional outreach: training members on how to discuss their faith and staffing the various community giveaways with faith sharers. The pastor was a talented athlete, competing in marathons and triathlons. Her knowledge of healthy eating could have been a powerful connecting point for a community that struggled with good food choices. Her biracial family status also fit well with the multicultural, diverse neighborhood. What holds someone back from leveraging their own situation to connect with the people right in front of them? I was hired by the denomination as a short-term coach to help this person develop their worship skills. She needed more in-depth coaching on outreach and faith sharing. My take is that her faith had not yet developed. If it were, she would have recognized the incredible fit she was for her location, and she would have been able to leverage those gifts beyond church walls to gather people who wanted her leadership in their lives.

Redefining the Boundaries

When churches undertake outreach and learn the sequence, they often become excited about the part involving large-scale events. Churches love those because they see them as not having to get so personal in the way of faith sharing. The church still operates under the assumption that new people will show up if the church does enough advertising and if the event is "in the pocket" of local culture.

I'll never forget the day a client called me to discuss the big plan for her church. She was the point person for the new service the church was starting. This young woman excitedly told me about the marathon they were hosting. The marathon wasn't a bad idea. But they were planning for it to occur in six weeks. That's about the time I stopped listening to what she said because none of it mattered. I started asking her questions she couldn't answer, like who was going to organize it, and how many people would they need to staff it, and what other things were going on in the community at that time, and were they going to use it to raise money, and how were they going to get people to participate in it, and what results were they seeking?

The only question she could answer was the one about the results. She said they were hoping to expose the community to the values of the church. That's when the conversation opened. The rest is history.

The point person went back to her team, and they regrouped. The church already had some involvement in the local food pantry, and they had a bus. They put together a food truck rally giveaway, redesigning their bus as a food truck and inviting a couple of other food trucks to participate as well. They also collected food for the food pantry. The physical weight of the food they collected was enormous. Their fun new worship band was there playing secular music. They staffed the rally with persons trained in faith sharing and outreach. They got quite a few names for their mailing list. They raised thousands of dollars from within their existing faith community for local neighborhood social service organizations. All of that was exactly who this church was meant to be. About five hundred people from the neighborhood made their way there. One member said to my client, "Wow, I don't know anyone here." My client responded, "That's the point."

Boundaries?

I coach a pastor who is a natural-born networker and incredibly good at developing community connections. He's just plain creative in how he engages the community to suit his church's needs. You can translate that statement into a monetary value. Such community connections have helped his smaller, older church not just stay afloat, but thrive. The problem is that when we first got connected, there was no observable structure or primary identity that the church could point to and say, "Look at this connection we have. This is who we are." Most declining churches are going in too many directions. Outreach in the mission field is more effective when a church acts according to its size. When you're smaller, you might only need one standout connection to effectively communicate with new people about who you are. That connection can be, "We're the church that teaches faith development." That's an excellent place to start being the church.

- Coaching stories reflection questions:
- What points did the stories raise?
- Did any describe you or your church? How?

II. Backstories of Institutionalism

Insights into the opening coaching stories

The stories you just read depict aspects of outreach specifically oriented toward church planting. They get the church out into the neighborhood to be noticed for what the church is doing as the church. We will focus on developing such events in part II, phase 3. Look ahead if you wish! Developing larger events is more demanding than you might think!

The key takeaway from the opening stories is that your church will use the secular culture to grow. That will present challenges to you. You'll have to determine where your line in the sand is. It will help if you know who you are.

Drawing your line in the sand

A line in the sand for a church preparing to do outreach is a boundary for what you're willing to do and not do. When you are a disciple who makes disciples, you are interacting in secular culture. It's appropriate to use the secular culture to communicate countercultural truths. In fact, it's required. The church can't be the church without using the culture to remain countercultural. Most people who became Christians did so within the framework of their daily lives—not behind church walls. All the faith stories in chapter 4 developed apart from the institutional church. If a church isn't willing to find ways to use the culture to remain countercultural, it remains isolated and thus institutional.

That said, it's also true that churches must discern what is too far. For many mainliners, it goes too far to give away a car to get people in the door. So they won't do that. That's their line in the sand. The question is, What will they do? You must know who you are and why you're making the decisions you're making. All of it will affect your growth. It should. You will be the size you are meant to be by putting all the pieces in place to reach more people with your unique perspective, gifts, style, context, and location. That's by God's design.

If you're going to pursue outreach, think of how you could use the secular culture to express yourself as yourself, not in trying to be someone else. Places where you could draw a line in the sand include:

Style

You'll hear a lot of well-known and effective pastoral leaders talk about "dressing like the mission field." From that perspective, many pastors could use a makeover. How far would you be willing to go to get one? It could help you fit into your mission field. That raises a question: Do you know your target? If you don't, then don't change your style yet. Or you could ask yourself: Do we have the right target if I need to change my style?

In the first story on conflict in chapter 3, the pastor described himself as a nerd. I got to know the pastor well. He was not stylish in dress or looks. But he had a huge heart for God and was incredibly smart. He found a place where he fit in and where his self-described nerdiness was an asset.

Let's say, though, that you do need to get the makeover. Would you get some new duds? Would you go on a fitness regime to trim down? Consider working with a personal trainer to get more fit, or a personal shopper to develop your look? Would you go to a bar to talk to someone about faith, wearing your biker jacket? Would you have to buy a biker jacket? Do you need some tattoos? Would you imbibe while at the bar, talking to your mission field? Would you drink alternative suds and be okay with your person drinking an adult beverage? Would you cuss? If you don't want to cuss, is it okay if others do? Where is your line in the sand?

Capacity

The fourth opening story in this chapter illustrates the church's capacity for outreach work. Your church will only reach a certain number of people, based in part on its size, when you first begin to learn and implement outreach. It's wise to assess your capacity line to know what you can realistically accomplish in the mission field. A church of 350 can bring a high-quality band and project videos on the jumbotron of the local university football stadium for a community-wide Easter sunrise service. A small church of about 50 people could gather lakeside near the local forest preserve that faces east to watch the sunrise and lead well-known, spiritual yet secular songs and familiar hymns with just one acoustic guitar and an amp, or maybe not even the amp. Both churches can discuss the supernatural power of God — one over a PA system, the other with a mic on the amp, or simply in their normal voices. Both gatherings can be well staffed with a healthy percentage of members who know outreach to make solid connections that lead to more solid connections. Many smaller churches often envy larger churches. Being true to who you are is more genuine.

The line in the sand is not trying to be the big church if you're a smaller church. That value is going to impact every church, and particularly the range of church sizes under 250 in worship that this material is geared toward. Has your church ever tried to emulate another church rather than staying true to its own identity?

Belief

The second of the opening stories tells the tale of a gifted person who struggled to connect her gifts and talents to the place where she was serving. The questions you must always ask about outreach are, Am I called to it? Am I called to it here? Am I in this place for such a time as this? Belief is a countercultural phenomenon. Do you fully believe that God is leading you to reach out? That belief changes everything. It is the one thing that allows you to see how God created you and thus to do the work to which God has called you. It's a fun question to ask people what they would have done vocationally if they hadn't done what they did. Personally, I can't see myself doing anything else because God has wired me missionally.

What is the central understanding you have of yourself that would change anything you do so that you'd wind up doing precisely what you are already doing? Why wouldn't you use the gifts God gave you to produce relevant ministry in your setting?

Disagreement

Drawing a line in the sand with your values is one of the most enduring lines between the church and the mission field. If "sharing the gospel message," like the church in the first story, is where you're at in reaching out to new people, then your approach is more transactional: Do something to get people to show up, then give them something they really need, according to your understanding of church life. If your outreach approach is more relational, then you're going to make personal contacts to build connections and not be as concerned about people hearing a gospel message but instead meeting Jesus through your experiences. Those approaches are vastly different from each other.

Except that even relational evangelism uncovers topics of disagreement between the church and the mission field. If you think your church is right about certain aspects of church life and the mission field disagrees with you, is there any way to build a faith community that embraces the differences while still pursuing Jesus side by side? If, for example, your church still struggles with LGBTQ+, can you still welcome gay and trans guests without judgment? What are other examples of something the church you serve may need to get past to welcome the emerging mission field?

The church doesn't have to agree with everything in culture to accept it. That could be a big learning curve for the church. Community is very important in the development of worship. And you can have community between disagreeing factions, even though it's challenging. Not everyone thinks the same. To strive to be a diverse church is not limited to demographic diversity, but also lifestyle. What about diversity of thought? How do you build an environment that's okay with disagreement?

Being truthful about your line in the sand (so maybe that's not your line)

The church featured in the opening story is a source of significant disagreement among most mainliners. A church that aims to "share the gospel message to offer salvation" is typically an evangelical, charismatic church. Sharing the gospel message means something specific: that someone will say yes to Jesus by receiving the gospel message of salvation and thereby be personally saved. Most mainliners don't think that way about Jesus. So a mainline church wouldn't give a big-ticket item away to get people in the door. And they might also be disdainful toward the church that did. A mainliner might wonder why a church would need to entice someone to hear about Jesus. You might wonder whether the person will return the big-ticket item once they're saved.

Fair enough. Except that most mainline churches offer giveaways to attract people to their doors. It just doesn't look like the church featured in the opening story because that church's big-ticket items are so . . . well . . . big, and the giveaways in mainline churches are more modest. Almost every church I've ever coached has a Trunk or Treat celebration. They give away a very precious, though relatively cheap, commodity (compared to a car): candy! They lure the kids and their parents with promises of fun and safety on Halloween. The church is stoked about all the people who showed up at the attractional event, even though the church has no idea who the people are, and not one of the new people who showed up for Trunk or Treat also show up on Sunday during worship.

Could you apply the term "institutional" to the "give-away" approach, regardless of the size of the giveaway? The expectation remains for "them" to come to "us." It would be countercultural for the church to staff the Trunk or Treat event with faith sharers to improve the capture rate. Much more authentic.

Does the third coaching story come closer to what you want to be?

The food truck rally featured in story three was a true countercultural expression. The church drew a line in the sand by making their event missional, relational, and representative of the church's values, rather than just hosting an event with no missional purpose beyond gaining recognition. This was a wealthy, mid-sized, very progressive church in a thriving suburb. They valued the service and care of the poor above all else. The church used the culture of food to say to the five hundred guests, "You can have great food here as long as you provide a similar meal for someone who can't afford it." It is countercultural to use the culture (food and sharing meals) to be countercultural (giving away food). How could your church do something like that at a scale that your church can handle?

Backstories reflection questions

1. Say why what you just read was:
    - surprising,
    - engaging,
    - confusing,
    - encouraging, or
    - concerning.
2. Where did you see your church in what you read?
3. Where did you see yourself?
4. Who were you thinking about in what you just read?
5. What are you going to do next?

III. Rewriting the Story of Your Church's Future

Drawing the line in the sand when you do outreach is inevitable. Churches can welcome all people, but not everyone will attend. That's the meaning of public worship. Everyone is welcome. However, not everyone will like what you do. To be intentional is to be faithful. It's a line in the sand that shows your trust in God to create the environment that is authentic for you. Those who relate to that environment could follow you a long way. Those who don't need a different church that they can fit into.

Countering Culture

31. What's your stance on …
32. Discern what's next
32. Consider demographics

One week to one month

In this chapter, you'll notice there aren't many to-dos. There are primarily considerations. Many mainline churches struggle to draw a clear line in the sand, particularly progressives who often seem reluctant to articulate their beliefs, fearing they may no longer remain inclusive. Evangelicals and charismatics don't have that problem. Mainliners can learn from them. We can embrace clarity too. I'll go out on a limb and say God seems diverse. God is in so many churches of so many different styles that receive a standard message: God is real, and following Jesus transforms us. How that is expressed differs from church to church and can alter how the message is conveyed. Growth is local. God is alive in all such localities.

At the end of this chapter, there will be one completed chart that represents all the tasks and to-dos in part I of this material. If you discern to go forward into part II, you'll be starting from a position of strength if you have accomplished all the tasks of part I, which is phase 1 of part II.

31. What is your church's stance on . . .

Hot-button topics

A way for churches to become authentic is to be clear about their stance on hot-button topics. The reason the topic is a hot button is that even the church struggles to understand its meaning. One such topic is salvation. At some point, the public you can reach will want to know what eternal life and salvation mean to you. We touched upon an evangelical perspective: Accept Jesus as your Lord and Savior, or be damned to everlasting hell. But that's not the only way to explain salvation. Others might say that salvation is being saved from yourself and your foibles through the eternal hope and peace that Jesus provides.

LGBTQ+ is at the head of the list of hot-button topics. Politics seems important. Some people in seats agree with being told how to vote. Others would not want to tie politics to Christianity. I've heard quite a bit from younger people in the mission field that they don't like how much of the country seems to equate Christianity with voting a certain way.

So what do you think about that preface? Say so here.

Conversion

The concept of conversion brings us back to the three church-planting categories of growth from the previous chapter, specifically the last: 5–10 percent of new converts. Converts?

If you do the type of outreach we're talking about in these pages, that is, pray that God will open the door to faith talk, you're bound to meet up with someone who has not connected with Jesus, ever. If you connect with them well and they express a desire to learn more about Jesus, you may need to help them verbally agree to follow Jesus. Can you really do that without offering a heaven-and-hell dichotomy?

Yes. There's something about saying out loud that you want to pursue faith that changes you, even if it isn't directly saying that you want Jesus to be your Lord and Savior. Saying that you want to pursue faith through Christianity is still a commitment and can be a type of conversion for someone who hasn't previously committed to that journey.

So what do you think about conversion? Say so here.

Saying it out loud

I had been ordained already when I went on staff at a mainline megachurch that was charismatic and evangelical. They have since left their tribe because of their stance on LGBTQ+ issues. They were still a perfect church for me to learn from in many ways, despite what turned out to be dividing lines. When I first went on staff, I observed how many non-ordained people in seats knew how to read the Bible with meaning. I wanted to learn that too. I asked the faith development pastor about it. She thought pairing me up with a layperson would help. The first and only time that layperson and I ever got together, I told her I was having trouble understanding the Bible. She asked me right then if I had ever really accepted Jesus into my heart. Well, of course I had! I had already had a relationship with Jesus. And I was ordained! She said, "But did you ever say the words out loud that you wanted Jesus as your savior?" Well, no. I hadn't. So my new friend walked me through what is known as "the sinner's prayer." And I asked Jesus to be my savior. Because, I said, I needed one. It was as if someone had flipped a switch. I have become very comfortable reading scripture since then. You could agree with the layperson and say that I grew comfortable with scripture because I confessed I'm a sinner, and took Jesus as my personal savior. I have very little trouble confessing my sins. And I love Jesus. And it didn't hurt me to say Jesus is my Lord. But to this day, I don't believe it was the Jesus as Lord language that helped me turn the corner. It was the overt, out-loud confession that told anyone who was listening that I wanted more, including God and also me.

Saying out loud that you want to follow Jesus is what is important. Romans 10:9 (CEB) says, "Because if you confess with your mouth 'Jesus is Lord' and in your heart you have faith that God raised him from the dead, you will be saved." "Because if," where this passage begins, could be a big "if." For churches that struggle to understand or define salvation, this passage might be perceived as divisive. Yet the "confessing with your lips" part still stands. There is something about uttering the words out loud that convinces you of what you are thinking.

We've been saying that about faith sharing throughout this book. When you, the faith sharer, reach out to tell someone else why you follow Jesus, you're reinforcing your own understanding of why. Others may hear it, but that's not your job to know. You just have to say it. And God reinforces your own belief in you for sure, even if it's not in God's timing to change the person you're talking to.

So what do you think about proclaiming faith out loud? Say so here.

Saying yes

Saying what you want to do out loud is the conversion part. Someone I mentored and coached for several years went on to become a worship leader at another church and developed a huge ministry. When she and I first got connected, I knew she wasn't yet as serious a Christian as she could be. Several months later, I noticed a change in her, especially as she began writing music that was both spiritually profound and singable, with a pop style. She told me that one day she was sitting in church and decided to whisper to Jesus to ask Jesus into her heart. That's an out-loud confession that had nothing to do with overtly saying you're a sinner.

In a conversation with a friend from my retail days, my friend raised concerns over the direction of the church in the twenty-first-century culture. She expressed a deep offense at the idea that so many Christians feel they have certain rights that not everyone else has. I share her concerns and was able to express them honestly to her. And then I was able to paint a picture of Jesus who doesn't demand, but instead offers, as Andrew said to his brother, "Come and see" (John 1:39). No pressure. Do you want to pursue that, Jesus, I asked her. Her yes is a profoundly life-changing confession.

Those who genuinely want to grow as disciples will likely meet with the tentative and possibly even the never-churched person somewhere along the line. Be ready to help them openly ask.

So what does it mean to say yes to Jesus? Say so here.

Stories of unbelief

Inclusiveness in our modern-day culture is about more than race and sexual identity. As already mentioned, it's also likely to be about diversity of thought. If you're creating community with the non-churched or lesser-churched culture, you'll find a variety of beliefs in things that equate to unbelief in the church and Jesus. Engaging new people in church who aren't yet fully committed to church life is a powerful testimony to your church's understanding of who God is.

When you share stories of unbelief in your faith community among stories of belief, you will find that some people will want to know more because of the discrepancy and transparency. When they say out loud that they want to give Jesus a try, even to see what you're talking about, it's a turning point. That's a good thing.

So what are the stories of unbelief that you can encourage in your church? Say so here.

32. Discern what's next

Will you proceed to part II? That means launching a new service or relaunching an existing worship service. You'll track numbers throughout the launch process to add new people to worship and reach a critical mass, thereby sustaining your gathering. You'll conduct outreach through faith sharing in the manner you learned in this part of the book. But you'll do it systematically, following a plan and a clear launch timeline. Look ahead to part II to see what's involved, if you haven't already.

What do you think?

33. Consider demographics

If you're pursuing outreach in your neighborhood toward some launch of worship through part II of this material, you'll need to be clear about your target. You can look ahead to the targeting entry in part II, phase 2. The entry is titled "Clarify Target."

Targeting is also an area of pushback for many church people. You'll often hear members say that everyone should be welcome at your church. Fair enough. But will all who are welcome want to be there? The answer is no. The entry on "Subjective Authenticity" from chapter 2 is worth the reread to help explain why.

Even with that explanation, targeting is a hurdle for members. It's counterintuitive to understand that diversity emerges through relationships, not attraction. The latter creates homogeneity, which is what most churches are experiencing now. "To target" means being intentional about growth. It's a recognition that God is the one making the connections between the church and the mission field, through church members.

For now, ask yourself these questions. Jot your notes to answer what you ask:

- Who has my heart stirred for while out walking or driving?
- What's the age range of those I relate to best?
- What is the economic status of those I relate to best?
- How would that group fit into our existing church?
- What does our demographic study indicate about that group?
- Are there any people in our church now who match that group?
- Where does the group of people live for whom I find my heart stirring?
- Does anyone in our church live near that group?
- What does our church want people to know about Jesus and the church?
- Does my/our Christian message cut through the noise our mission field is hearing?
- How do we need to reframe the message to cut through the noise?
- Can we reframe the message?

Now write out a short statement of a few sentences about your target that includes the following:

- age,
- economics,
- education level,
- your primary message about Jesus and the church, and
- how you'll communicate that message.

Begin sharing components of this description of your target with those considering participating in the launch process in part II. You'll likely receive additional input from launch team participants. See if you missed anything or see if they missed anything. Hold findings loosely until you have a chance to clarify what you're doing in part II.

Rewriting your story reflection questions

1. Say why what you just read was:

    - surprising,
    - engaging,
    - confusing,
    - encouraging, or
    - concerning.

2. Where did you see your church in what you read?

3. Where did you see yourself?

4. Who were you thinking about in what you just read?

5. Additional chapter questions:

    - How does the church remain countercultural by using the culture to communicate with the mission field?
    - Where is your church the vaguest about who you are and how can you address that?

6. What are you going to do next?

Chapter Postscript

If you discern that you're going to pursue outreach in part II to transform existing worship or start something new, then it's time for two things. One is the conversation with your board that you considered in chapter 1. Return to that chapter/entry to see what you wrote and thought about your board.

The other is the possible appointment of someone to carry this process forward is outlined in part II of this material. The closer your church is to 250 in worship, the more critical it is to consider hiring or appointing someone to lead your worship project forward. Developing a point person for worship will help stretch churches that currently average about 100 people in worship each week. If your church has fewer than 100 in worship, the pastor will likely lead the process forward into part II of this material. Those insights provide a starting point for the conversation with your board.

If the pastor is going to lead the project, plan to devote approximately five to ten hours per week to developing part II. Have you streamlined your schedule yet? Can you do it again or more? I work with many pastors who take on part II, and it's busy, but manageable. It doesn't take as many hours for a pastor of a smaller congregation to pursue part II as it would be for a pastor of a larger one, or even as it would be for a new hire.

If you're going to appoint someone to take on the development of a new faith community, you could be looking at a part-time position. It will take longer for a new hire than for someone already engaged in your church. Should that be your focus, consider the job description in what follows.

Job description for a point person for your launch process

II

a. Duties

- Engage and grow the launch team.
- Lead the project from 0 to critical mass.
- Interact in the mission field personally.
- Start groups.
- Launch the service/faith community.
- Continue to lead and develop the community after launch.
- Becoming familiar with *Rebuilding In-Person Worship* values and processes.

b. Hours and pay

- Salaried is best.
- The salary range is local. Research to determine a figure that will attract high-quality candidates.
- Plan for, at minimum, a half-time position for starting an entirely new service.

c. Target

- Know and articulate your target in the job description.
- Articulate the need for affinity between point person, the target, and the existing faith community.
- Emphasize faith sharing as the focus.

d. Bi-vocational

- A start-up leader could be employed in the marketplace half-time and make numerous connections to support the start-up process.

Discerning Your Role	Leading Worship	Expecting Pushback	Growing Comfortable With Faith-Talk	Doing The Math	Countering Culture
1. Increase spiritual practices 2. Expect resistance (to #1) 3. Discern your role 4. Address your schedule 5. Establish a timeline 6. Go public 7. Gather participants 8. Start or transform worship 9. Prepare talk/ count cost 10.See fruit	IMPLEMENT 11. Worship leader dynamics 12. Space dynamics 13. Flow dynamics 14. Confessional (interactive) prayer 15. Sermon prep community	16. Gather intercessors 17. Pursue Mt. 18 18. Come to Jesus 19. Preach on conflict 20. Do prayer walks	21. Learn from others' stories 22. The Fatih Story Alphabet 23. F.R.A.N.C. 24. Pursue outreach strategies 25. Pursue your story 26. Make videos	27. Critical mass for your service 28. Launch team numbers 29. Contacts and connections 30. Organizing a digital faith community	31. What's your stance on … 32. Discern what's next 33. Consider demographics
One to four weeks	**One to many weeks**	**One month to many weeks**	**One week to one month**	**One week to one month**	**One week to one month**

Part I Postscript

When I lead teaching cohorts for church leaders on rebuilding in-person worship, I help them learn how to prepare to teach the material to their congregations effectively. Some leaders drop out before gathering their people for a study because of the cohort. They didn't realize what this material represented before. Some want to continue, but are concerned that their people won't opt in. If you've previewed the material and now it's time to introduce it to your people, but you're timid, the question is, Have you been praying? How are you doing with your intercessors? Have you addressed your schedule? You don't have to quit even if you have the urge.

If you decide to continue by starting your own teaching cohort within your church to make your way through Part I, consider the short teaching plan on the next page. Then fast forward to the Phase I postscript in Part II for some thoughtful questions to ask yourself as a leader, so that you can impart knowledge and purpose to participants in your study and to your entire congregation if you're the pastor.

Teaching plan

Assignment	Steps for the session	Time alloted
-Read the chapter -Answer all questions -Come to sesh prepared to: 1. Talk about one answer 2. Ask one question	1. Ice breaker You will need an icebreaker for the first 2 to 3 sessions	10 minutes
	2. Overview Your takeaways from the chapter and the main points that you think are important for your people to grasp	10 minutes
	3. Discussion of their answers and questions	15 minutes
	4. Tasks	35 minutes
	5. Reminder for assignment, then pray out	5 minutes

Seven-week cohort option

- Week One: Intro and chapter one
- Week Two: Chapter Two
- Week Three: Chapter Three
- Week Four: First half of Chapter Four
- Week Five: Meet individually with study participants
- Week Six: Second half of Chapter 4 and first half of Chapter 5
- Week Seven: Second half of Chapter 5 and Chapter 6, and next steps

What to talk with study participants about in your one-on-one

What they've learned, where they are in their journey, what they want to see the church accomplish in worship and outreach, how they see their own role developing in becoming a disciple-making disciple.

Length of study sessions

75 minutes, except for week seven, which is 90 minutes

Expected outcome of seven-week study, plans for:

1. Teaching key concepts to the congregation over time, and repeated over time.
2. Completing tasks for all the groundwork
3. Moving into Part Two, or not
4. Confirming a possible commitment from some who want to pursue outreach

Icebreakers for weeks one, two, and three, if you need them

1. Name of your favorite pet and why it is your favorite pet
2. Favorite concert you ever went to and why it was your favorite
3. The biggest conflict you ever had and how you resolved it

Part II

OUTSIDE YOUR BUILDING

Phase One

LAY GROUNDWORK

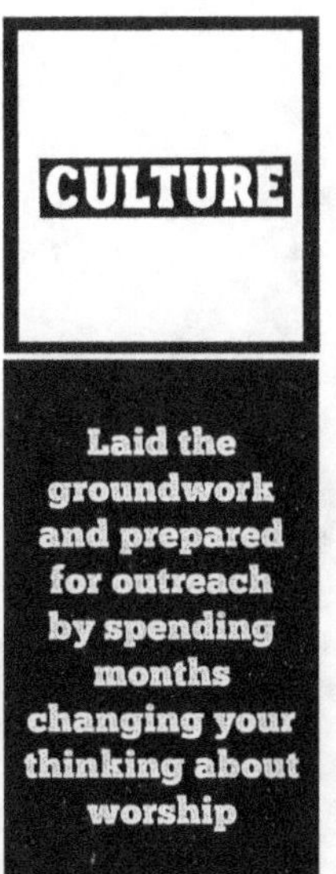

Phase One Notes

Good news! You've already completed phase 1 of part II of *Rebuilding In-Person Worship*! Phase 1 of part II is the entirety of part I of this workbook. If you've done all the tasks associated with Laying groundwork, you're in a good position to begin part II.

In part I, you changed your thinking about worship and worship growth. In part II, you'll change your behavior to pursue outreach and launch a new service or relaunch an existing one. The launch process helps you grow numerically. But the launch process is built on faith sharing. Your primary behavior change is not just recognizing that you have a faith story but also that you'll begin to share it beyond church walls and into everyday life. Your goal as a faith community is to share enough stories to make enough connections with new people that in-person worship will transform. You are in a position of strength to move forward. You're rebuilding in-person worship!

Phase One:
Lay Groundwork

Step / task
1

All Of
Part One

In
Rebuilding In-Person Worship

2 to 6 months

You've been on a steep learning curve through part I. You're beginning part II about ⅓ to ½ of the way up that curve. Good thing you've bought some climbing shoes; the prayer is to continue following God into the mission field.

Phase One Postscript

The thing is, you haven't really started part II yet. You laid the groundwork, but you are not yet committed until you have your point person and your launch team in place. This is the time to take more time to discern and maybe also complete part I if you haven't yet. You have likely made some significant movement in worship development by pursuing the part I study. And, as frequently noted, you'll drop back from enthusiasm and people if you don't hit play to move forward into the next phase of part II. But if God is with you, then God is in this with you. You can hit pause if needed. God won't leave. God will still want you to move toward deeper faith by making new disciples. In that way worship thrives, and worship is God's deal. This book, the purpose of the church, and following God into the mission field will be waiting for you. When you're ready. . . .

Phase Two

FORM LAUNCH TEAM

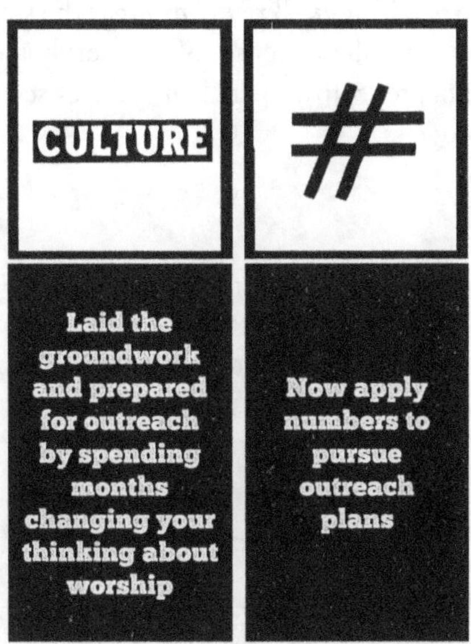

Phase Two Notes

You gathered participants for the part I study. They were not your launch team—the group of people who agree to pursue faith sharing in the mission field systematically to launch or relaunch a worship service. The part I participants served as your test market to learn what it would take to pursue faith sharing beyond church walls so that you could rebuild in-person worship. You may have already noticed some impact on in-person worship because of your initial study and those who pursued it with you.

But it wasn't required that the initial study participants move into part II. If you're here now, at least one or a few of you likely agreed to continue. However, you may need to add a few new people to the launch team to have enough people to develop the launch process and reach critical mass. You'll form your launch team in phase 2, both numerically and spiritually, to strengthen your ability to launch well.

The "phase notes" in part II are like the "chapter notes" from part I. They provide direction to focus on the launch phase you're in (like a director would do in a play for the actors). The direction for this phase of your work is to become organized.

1. Start to Form a Launch Team

Refer to the review of the formula in entry #6 to determine the number of participants required to initiate your launch process. Follow the engagement process for adding new people to the launch team, found in entry #12.

Bring new participants up to speed

Adding new people to your launch team at this stage doesn't mean you have to take more people through the study you just completed. Provide workbooks for them to work through part I on their own, paying special attention to chapter 4. Include new participants in the online faith community you developed in part I. Follow this process with everyone you add to the launch team as you go.

Hit Benchmarks (make new disciples who make new disciples)

One feature you've noticed of *Rebuilding In-Person Worship* is the storyboard. You can follow the action by reading all the storyboard entries. The phase 2 entry of the storyboard in part II says, "then apply numbers for making outreach plans." Chapter 5 from part I introduces several growth formulas. Refer to that chapter frequently to check your progress.

Phase Two:
Form Launch Team

2. Calendar - personalize & read ahead
3. Engage a coach
4. Confirm target
5. Set critical mass
6. Review the math
7. Match members
8. Set schedule- launch date
9. Plan gathering
10. Write descript.-A
11. Write descript.-B
12. Recruit the launch team
13. Design tools
14. List contacts
15. Host gathering
16. Begin outreach
17. Adjust calendar

Increase prayer
Share faith

2 to 4 months

Overcome Institutionalism

- The backstory for part II is part I.
- All of part II is behavior change.
- Behavior change is how you'll overcome institutionalism in your church.
- All of part II is about overcoming institutionalism.

Tasks abound in part II. Meetings with your launch team do not. Engage launch team participants in conversations about their progress with new behaviors through individual mentoring and within the online faith community. In-person meetings are for specific training and encouragement. Otherwise, the time it will take for launch team members to stay in connection with the person they're praying for will wane.

The timeline for part I is nine to eighteen months to reach launch, including phase 1. Rushing might cause you to skip steps, which will impede the goal of reaching critical mass. Taking too long risks a sense of languishing and member attrition.

Changes to the phase (chapter) structure to notice in the step-up chart include:

- Phases, not chapters. The chapters in part I helped you change your thinking. The phases in part II are directive and prescriptive. When you complete the phase, you should see progress to propel you into the next phase.
- Calendaring. The leader creates a plan and brings the launch team along. Every task listed in the step-up column goes on the calendar, and then some.
- Increase prayer, share faith. Keep doing those things even when you're down.
- Return to worship. Continue to share insights from your journey into public worship leadership in the mission field. See the chapter postscript for nuances. 

2. Calendar—personalize and read ahead

The launch team leader has a lot to organize. One organizational tool is the step-up chart, along with its accompanying entries. Another is the calendar you make, which is new in part II. The calendar is a tool to help you develop and stick to your plan.

A. Making and Sticking to Your Plan

- The leader plans.
- The leader helps the launch team stay on track with the plan.
- The calendar helps the leader keep the launch team on track.
- If the plan goes off the rails, you're in trouble with your launch.
- Being in trouble with your launch means you probably aren't going to reach critical mass, which means you might not be able to launch—or not launch well.
- If you launch but don't achieve critical mass, the likelihood of post-launch growth is slim.
- Being in trouble with your launch can trigger a lot of emotion and possibly rebellion, given the significant investment everyone has made so far.
- Put enough detail into the calendars to keep you on track.
- Stick to the plan.

B. Effective Calendaring. The focused leader will:

1. Read ahead. Preview the steps and tasks in detail for the phase you're in, and skim entries in upcoming phases to identify what needs a jump start.
2. Personalize the calendar. Include things on the calendar that will slow your pace (e.g., spouse's birthday dinner; confirmation retreat).
3. Make an initial phase 2 calendar. See the sample calendar below.

1 Calendar - read ahead	2 Confirm target	3	4	5	6 Set critical mass	7
8	9 Review Math Match members	10 Plan Gathering	11 Write description-a Write description-b	12 Recruit team	13 Design tools	14
15 Engage coach	16	17	18	19	20 Confirmation retreat →	21
22	23	24 Host Gathering	25 Begin outreach	26	27	28 Calendar adjustments

C. Components of the Sample Calendar

1. Provide a hand-drawn resource. Get your markers and sticky notes, plus flip-chart paper in landscape position, and draw your one-month calendar.
2. Transfer tasks from the step-up chart. One task per sticky note.
3. List a guesstimate. How long will it take to complete one task? Leave one to more days between that sticky note and the next one based on your projections.
4. Include more tasks. The confirmation retreat isn't listed on the step-up chart, but it will still require your time, so it should be added to the calendar.
5. Make it detailed. The sample calendar is just that. It's not as thorough as you can and probably should make your own if you're going to stick to your plan.
6. Make it visible. Remind everyone that it's on your office wall and that they can look at it even when you're not there (because you're in the mission field making contacts and sharing faith!).

3. Engage a coach

Although this material is written to help leaders do this work independently, part II can become a bit challenging. An outside voice can help you navigate the hurdles and stumbling blocks on your learning climb up the steep hill, allowing you to stay on track with hitting benchmarks to reach a critical mass. Individual and group coaching are standard coaching options. Author-led coaching offers both options.

- Individual coaching: Your church can engage a coach who helps you focus on your project by tailoring the coaching process to your specific needs. Individual coaching is more expensive, but even smaller churches often use it because they can obtain a grant.
- Group coaching: Teaching-coaching cohorts can be highly effective for churches exploring this material and not yet ready to fully adopt it in their church. Cohort-based coaching is much less expensive than individual coaching. When churches decide to pursue behavioral change by sharing their faith beyond church walls, cohort-based coaching can fill the bill, especially for smaller churches. The downside is that you don't receive a customized coaching approach tailored to your individual project. The benefits can outweigh that deficit, depending on your situation.

4. Confirm target

Most mainline groups subscribe to some demographic reporting. Someone in your church is good at understanding those studies and interpreting them. What most leaders don't exactly know how to do is apply the studies to a launch process. That's what you'll learn in this entry.

A. Targeting and Demographic Studies, Conceptually

Begin by returning to part I, chapter 6, entry #33, Consider demographics. Reread your initial thoughts about who your target might be. Targeting is practical but it's also about your heart. God is in both aspects of the process.

Pause to deepen your understanding of the impact of affinity on who you can realistically reach out to as a church. Demographic studies reveal the largest demographic in your area. Churches often assume they should target that demographic because they believe it will attract more people. That's an institutional mindset. The question is, does this demographic have representation in our church? If so, then you might have a chance to connect. If not, connecting is much more difficult. Churches exhibit the same mindset when they claim to want "the young people." However, the demographic study indicates that there aren't many in the area. Or even if there are, the church's average age is over seventy. Making connections with twenty- or thirty-somethings isn't realistic.

A better approach to using a demographic study for launch is not to target the largest demographic in your area mindlessly. Instead, use the study for launching.

B. Using a Demographic Study for Launching

1. Start with prayer walks (part I, chapter 3).
2. Generate a demographic study for your area.

   - for one to three and five-mile radius around your church in a high-density population area (urban);
   - five-ten-twenty miles around your church in a lower-density population (suburban to rural);
   - if there are barriers to accessing your building, such as a highway, a train track, or a forest/park/recreation area, draw a polygon, not a radius. Exclude the side of the map that includes the train tracks and related features from your polygon.

3. Study traffic patterns.

    - Where do people live? Identify neighborhoods.
    - Plot the traffic flow when someone drives from their home in their neighborhood to go to work, school, shopping, or the gym.
    - Does the traffic flow go near your church? A person doesn't have to pass directly by your church for the traffic flow to benefit your church. Traffic flow benefits your church when people drive toward it to pursue everyday activities. It will also be normal for them to visit your church if they are interested.
    - Circle the neighborhoods from which residents will drive your way daily.

4. Discover if your area is growing or declining

    - Talk to Realtors, teachers, hospital workers, school principals, and local merchants. What can they tell you about why your area is growing or declining? The why provides a doorway for connecting.
    - What demographics live in the housing developments you've circled?
    - Does anyone in your church live in that neighborhood or match the demographic from that neighborhood?

5. Make a list of good mission field matches.

    - See entry 7 in part I, chapter 1, "Gather Participants."
    - Add the following new qualifications to that list. Do they:
        - o match the demographic, the lifestyle values, or something else?
        - o want to grow in faith and discipleship?
        - o grasp that outreach is key to worship development?
        - o talk about change or transformation of worship and the church?

By the time you launch, about 50 percent or more of your launch team will comprise new people who generally represent your target.

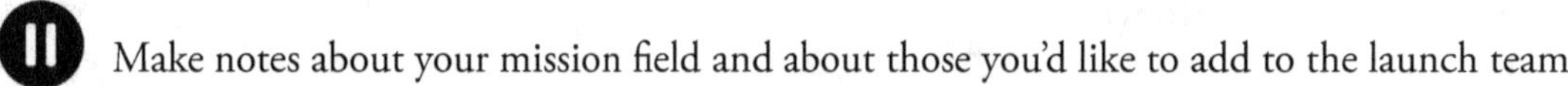

Make notes about your mission field and about those you'd like to add to the launch team.

Calendar when you'll start reaching out to new people in your church and when you'd like to be done recruiting from within.

5. Set critical mass

Reread the segments on critical mass in chapter 5 if there are any questions about what it is. You need a specific, hard number that you write down, which is the right number for the worship service you're developing to achieve social momentum.

Below is a synopsis of how to think about critical mass.

1. Critical mass of about fifty to seventy-five is likely in an area that has:

   - low population density, but it could be urban or a college town,
   - local gathering spots that cater to smaller crowds,
   - a "largest" Protestant church that may have their largest service of one hundred to two hundred, or
   - a hospital or clinic that never has a lot of cars in the lot at any given time.

2. Critical mass of about one hundred to two hundred is likely in an area that has:

   - high population density, and could be suburban;
   - popular restaurants that seat over two hundred when full and are about half to ¾ full for lunch;
   - hospitals or clinics in which the parking lot appears packed most of the day; or
   - evening rush hour traffic that's becoming big-city like.

Write some thoughts about your area. What's your critical mass number? Why are you leaning toward that number?

6. Review the math

Refer to part I, chapter 5, for a deeper understanding of the growth formulas to pursue. Two key formulas are below.

A. Overall Numbers

- Gather 10–12 percent of critical mass for your launch team (likely mostly members).
- Reach 3 × the original launch team size by the time of launch.
- Triple the tripled number through the actual launch (see phase 5).
- Make 20 × the critical mass number in contacts to reach critical mass.
- Make 10 × the 20 × critical mass number in connections to reach critical mass.
- Meet in a room that's about 30 percent bigger than critical mass.

B. Personal Outreach Plan Numbers per Launch Team Participant

- Eighty percent make ten contacts with one F.R.A.N.C. list person in nine months.
- Twenty percent make ten contacts with three persons in eighteen months.

- The leader personally makes ten-plus contacts to add thirty to forty new people in eighteen months.
- New launch team participants reach out to one person through launch.

Translate what you've read into your own language if it will be helpful for you to reach your benchmarks.

7. Match members

If you don't have a big enough launch team to start your launch process, you can add new people to it—members, nonmembers, and non-churched connections, or all of these—and work to match them to the mission field. See entry #4 to identify your mission field.

- To match the members to the mission field requires two values:
- realistic targeting, and
- a broad understanding of affinity.

A. Realistic targeting

It's common for churches to try to attract younger people. But how much younger? If your congregation's average age is seventy-five-plus you're not going to become a church of twenty-somethings suddenly. Three things will make targeting more realistic.

- One is to bring your target's age down by ten to twenty years, not fifty.
- Two is to connect over values, not just demographics. Return to chapter 6 to learn to articulate who your church is and what you stand for. An example of a lifestyle and missional church value is learning to share faith beyond church walls.
- Three is if the launch team leader is either younger than the average age of the launch team or perhaps is cross-cultural. Some leaders in their fifties still can connect with twenty-somethings and seventy-somethings.

B. Communicating values

In part I, we identified messaging as a key approach to communicating church values; review in chapter 2.

Other forms of messaging include social media posting and conversations over coffee with members and during meetings, also groups. Fast-forward to the next chapter to read entry #18.

The person you select as a worship leader or point person for your launch process will also represent your church's values and help draw participants together beyond demographics.

C. Combining Approaches

Pursue a realistic target that aligns with your demographic and simultaneously communicates your values.

Create an initial list of members who align with the mission field—calendar when you're going to reach out to them and how. When you reach out to them, they may respond with a yes, but they may also respond with a no. If they say no, ask if you can still connect with them to discuss the mission field from their perspective. Also, they might have friends that aren't engaged in church life that they may be willing to introduce you to. Return to the resource for community interviews at the end of chapter 4.

8. Set schedule (your launch date)

To set your launch date, calculate and project the amount of time you think it will take to complete tasks to get to critical mass. Then add the other factors below and work backward from the projected launch date to adhere to the recommended timelines in each phase of the step-up charts.

A. Total Number of Months

The launch date is expected to be approximately seven to fourteen months from now. You spent two to six months laying groundwork, and the total process takes nine to eighteen months. If you have launched before, you'll probably be at the shorter end of the timeline. If you haven't, it will take longer.

B. Geographic Location

- For northern-climate churches, a fall launch is optimal.
- For southern climate churches, you may have more leeway with the weather. Fall is still a good time because kids return to school.

C. Secular Celebrations

- You could tie a launch to the Super Bowl, for example. The spring real estate market kicks off in many climates just after the Super Bowl. Spring awareness is in the air for the secular culture, making that a good time to launch.
- You may have something local that significantly impacts your area. Seasonal fishing openers are very big in some local cultures, for example.
- Consider one of those dates based on the other information below.

D. Dates Following the Launch and Attendance Drop Off

- Attendance will drop after your launch, and you'll need to rebuild it.
- What dates come right after your projected launch date that could cause further attrition or that you could leverage to your advantage?

E. Four Weeks of Launch

- The launch is four weeks for optimal results. Consider all the above factors to determine the date that the fourth launch week represents for the various scenarios you've considered for your launch date.

F. Funding Variables

- If you need funding for technology, staff, or new hires, or improving your space in any way, and you haven't figured that out yet, factor it in now in your date planning.

G. Congregational Readiness

- A launch-ready congregation is one that has a cohesive launch team with mostly trained-in-faith-sharing participants who are pursuing their F.R.A.N.C. list and personal outreach plan, and a dedicated leader to guide them forward.
- A launch team that isn't as ready will need more time to pursue their F.R.A.N.C. list and to grow numerically with new people.
- You'll be developing a calendar to represent how much time you think it will take to complete all tasks with your existing launch team.

- Given all those factors, when is your specific launch? How might you have to reposition the sticky notes on your calendar?

9. Plan gatherings

You'll meet no more than four times in a nine- to eighteen-month launch timeline. Follow the script for each meeting below and add any additional information you think is necessary to encourage your group that isn't listed.

A. The First Gathering

1. Select a location: Select someone's home or the church building if needed.
2. Provide childcare: Pay childcare workers to be present to take care of kids; this would be an evangelism line item.
3. Don't do much with food.*
    - Food takes time to prepare—time that is better spent doing one-to-one outreach.
    - Only small gatherings have food. Your purpose is to grow. Keep your gathering small when you add food. So don't.
    - Do offer water, coffee, and soda.
    - Emphasis: Don't spend a lot of time or money on food. Churches don't take this seriously. Don't be that church!
4. Play recorded music as people gather.
5. Sing a couple of songs like those you'll use in worship, led by your worship leader or you can use a video.
6. Play a video of someone sharing their testimony.
7. The leader connects to the testimony, then does some teaching.
    - Review F.R.A.N.C. and personal outreach plans.
    - Share goals for the next several months.

- Go through the contact list.
- Introduce invitation tools (entry #13).
- Introduce the calendar (entry #17).
- Ask if there are questions about some of the activities on the to-do list.
- Promote the online faith community.
- Be clear about next steps.
- Provide the launch team with the dates for upcoming gatherings.
- Encourage the invitation of new people.

8. Leaving

- Sing a song, or not.
- Offer a blessing.
- Play recorded music as people leave.

B. Subsequent In-Person Gatherings

1. If you're making good progress:
   - Meet again in about six weeks.
   - Follow the above format.
2. If you need more group training, meet again in about four weeks.

C. Increasing the Size of Your Gatherings

- Add about 20 percent new people every time you gather in person.
- Consider the online faith community a place where you regularly add new people.
- All persons on your mailing list should be invited to participate in the online group. All who have engaged new people can invite them to the next gathering.

Make your meeting outline and all calendaring notes to keep you on track!

10. Write Description A

If you're adding anyone new to your launch team right now, you can provide them with a job description, as they haven't gone through part I of *Rebuilding In-Person Worship*. Continue to update the job description as you go, as you'll be adding new team members to the launch team until the launch.

- Launch Team Job Description
    - Purpose: to grow in faith and become part of the church's future through worship
    - Goals: learn outreach, gather new people, and improve in-person worship at our church
- Activities
    - Read *Rebuilding In-Person Worship.*
    - Learn how to write your personal testimony.
    - Get comfortable talking about faith with people you already know.
    - Pray for and reach out to people you already know.
    - Participate in an online group for prayer and teaching.
    - Gather for a couple in-person meetings of the launch team (with the dates).
    - Spend about two to three hours a week learning and developing outreach for about nine months.

Write your launch team participant job description!

11. Write Description B

Launch team participants will value a mission field description.

Sample Mission Field Description

Disenfranchised Mindy and Eli have been gone from church for at least a decade. They have a young family with one more on the way and want to get out of their starter home. They like outdoor activities, and they love the access to the trails in our nearby parks a new home would provide. They both have good jobs, and Mindy works from home. They are disenfranchised from the church because both saw their home churches split apart over what they thought were prejudicial issues. Eli's parents participate in our church and have told Eli about some good things in our church. Eli is considering participating here but isn't sure about Mindy, who is a gamer and who isn't as interested in pursuing church life as Eli is.

When you put your description together, be sure to include a statement about:

- the age and values of your target,
- their existing relationship to or value of (or lack of value) the church,
- their economic status,
- the growth or decline of your area,
- what might connect your target to your church, and
- other insights you find relevant (while keeping the description short!).

Write a description of your mission field—in pencil. You'll edit it along the way.

12. Recruit the launch team

A. Prayerfully Make a List of New People

- Match them to the mission field (see next entry).

B. Reach Out to Those on the List Individually

- Share what you've done so far in part I and outreach efforts, and what you've learned.
- Reveal your prayers for your invitee.
- Ask invitees to prayerfully consider growing in their own faith by learning to share their own faith story and improving the worship landscape in your church.
- Provide a job and mission field description.
- Provide a meeting schedule, with the first meeting scheduled two to four weeks prior to the end of phase 2.
- Provide copies of *Rebuilding In-Person Worship* and ask invitees to read the assigned sections.
- Offer to go through it with invitees for an hour or so, given that they weren't in the study, or pair them with someone who has gone through it if appropriate.
- Engage them in the online group even if they don't agree to be on the launch team.

C. Give them time to pray and respond

- Allow them time to get back to you about launch team participation.

13. Design tools

Consider invitation tools to increase engagement.

A client planned to provide suckers to students on a college campus that read "The Church That Doesn't Suck." A client was reaching out to bikers in a town where locals often went to a bar that gave out free shots. She wanted to give out shots there and say, "Give our church a shot." A megachurch put business cards in their bulletins that were artistically designed and featured upcoming sermon series plus contact info.

1. Cheesy-niche-plain. That describes the invite tools in sequence. All are effective, depending on your specific context.
2. Be ready. Bring invitation tool samples to the first in-person launch team gathering.
3. Who can design? Maybe someone on your launch team or even an artsy member who is not on the team.
4. Provide guidance. What's the ethos of your group? Who is your mission field? Those factors will influence design.
5. Not a substitute. The people on your launch team will have a personal outreach plan tied to their F.R.A.N.C. list. Invitation tools do not replace that plan.
6. Hand out freely. When talking to someone about faith, or not, a launch team participant can hand out an invitation tool.
7. Provide many. Each launch team participant should have lots of handouts.

Write down some ideas for invite tools that fit your context or plan to find someone who can do that (if not you).

14. List contacts

Another invitation tool is your contact list. Gathering names and increasing your list helps build momentum and fulfill some of the formulas from chapter 5. Consider the following information to include on your list.

- name
- cell phone
- email
- interests
- other connecting points
- interest level in our project

The last bullet would be observations you have made about your person, perhaps readiness for discipleship, or interest in serving in a particular area, or even reticence to what you're doing. Find a way to capture this information.

Design a contact form that all launch team participants (including you) can easily access when creating their own contacts.

15. Host gathering

You planned your gathering already, and now you're hosting it.

16. Begin outreach

You may have already started outreach. If not, you can wait until phase 3, or if some are ready to proceed now, encourage them to pursue their F.R.A.N.C. list. The leader is likely already engaged beyond church walls.

17. Adjust Calendar

Below is another sample calendar that shows how you might adjust your schedule to accommodate tasks that were not completed in the first month of the phase you're in. You'll move those from the first calendar to the second one.

Now include two more items.

- Tasks from part I that still need to be addressed.
- Planning for tasks that must be started now to complete them by the time you read them. When you read entries ahead that are in the next phase of your process (not the one you're in), note the new addition:

29	30	31	1	2	3
	(Yellow Sticky) *Task: Calendar and read ahead*		(Blue Sticky) *Task: Group Process*	(Yellow Sticky) *Task: Neighborhood*	
4	**5**	**6**	**7**	**8**	**9**
	(Blue Sticky) *Task: Large group event*	(Yellow Sticky) *Task: Finish recruit. L.T.*		(Yellow Sticky) *Task: Neighborhood*	(Pink Sticky) *Task: Intercessors*
10	**11**	**12**	**13**	**14**	**15**
(Pink Sticky) *Task: Sermon Prep Approach*		(Yellow Sticky) *Task: Reschedule host gathering*	(Green Sticky) *Task: College tours*	→	→
16	**17**	**18**	**19**	**20**	**21**
	(Yellow Sticky) *Task: Neighborhood*	(Blue Sticky) *Task: Worship hire*	(Pink Sticky) *Task: Worship flow*	(Yellow Sticky) *Task: Neighborhood*	
22	**23**	**24**	**25**	**26**	**27**
				(Green Stiky) *Task: B-day party*	

The sticky notes color indications represent the following:

- tasks listed in the step-up column
- ongoing or incomplete tasks from part I
- plan-ahead tasks from part II that you'll have to start now in order to complete them on time (The plan-ahead icon, on the right, flags plan-ahead entries in part II.) 
- personal or church activities that take time and need to be accounted for in your timeline

Phase Two Postscript

Be cautious when discussing the launch in existing worship. If you're starting a new service, members who aren't involved in the launch won't want to know how excited you are about projects that don't include them. If you're relaunching an existing worship service, members who aren't involved in the launch will take it personally when you're so excited about making changes. It's very important for leaders to publicly talk about their work in the mission field because all Christ followers are called to the same job and behavior. Don't talk about the launch. Discuss the people and how God is transforming you, the one who shares faith beyond church walls.

Phase Three

SHARE FAITH

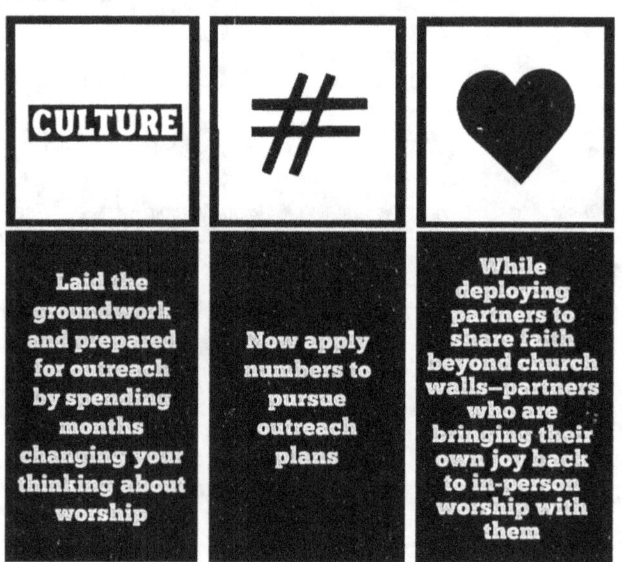

Phase Three Notes

Sharing your testimony is not the same as writing it. You climbed a steep learning curve to about ⅓ or ½ the height of the curve when you learned to write your testimony. You're still climbing the learning curve by sharing your story with friends, out loud!

Climbing a mountain can be scary, especially if you look back to see how steep it is. Pray for God to open the doorway to faith talk. That's how the mountain flattens out. When you climb to the next level, you'll look down onto the basecamp.

The climbing plan is to pursue the F.R.A.N.C. list. That's your harness. Trust.

18. Calendar—personalize and read ahead

Repeat the pattern from phase 2 to prepare for developing this phase of launching. Read ahead to determine which entries to pursue for immediate results and which to get a head start on, so you can complete them on time.

19. Follow F.R.A.N.C.

1. Review personal outreach plan. Part I, chapter 5.
2. Review the number of connections. Also, in chapter 5.
3. Implement the plan. Now is the time.
4. Study the plan one more time for implementation.

    - Make a F.R.A.N.C. list.
    - Select/discern one name to pray over.
    - Follow the 1-1-1-1 prayer for that person.
    - Make a list of activities to engage your person in that you normally do
    - Engage your person in one or more of those activities.
    - Pray before you participate.
    - Ask God to open the doorway to faith talk.
    - Practice your testimony before going.
    - Prepare to share a bit or more of your testimony when with your friend.
    - See where the conversation goes.
    - Schedule another time to get together.
    - Pray that God would open the doorway to faith talk.
    - See where it goes.
    - Possibly invite your person into a study or a group when the time is right.
    - Stay connected with a normal pace of repeating the activity with your friend.
    - Make plans to connect approximately ten times in nine months with one person.

Phase Three: Share Faith

18. Calendar - personalize and read ahead
19. Follow F.R.A.N.C.
20. Tap media
21. Form groups
22. Use online community
23. Plan-host events
24. Revisit in-person worship
25. Launch-team gathering
26. Hire worship leader
27. Revisit in-person worship-again
28. Adjust Calendar

Increase prayer
Share Faith

3 to 5 months

Make notes about F.R.A.N.C., and calendar.

20. Tap media

Social media could represent an emotional hurdle for some. This entry may help you think through how to manage usage.

1. Identify purpose (to engage social media users in discussions about faith).

2. Stay organized.

3. Everyone posts, including the leader.

4. Posts are:

    - Text-based: Writing only; a sentence or two.
    - Image-based: Pictures with a brief caption.
    - Video-based: Less than a minute or even thirty seconds, often with a transcription.
    - SHORT!

5. Create something like the five *P*s for content development:

    - Purpose: reinforcing the church's identity
    - Preaching: snippets from your message this past week (thirty seconds or less)
    - Personal: what "I'm" doing in life and the mission field
    - Prayer: front and center
    - Promoting: remind participants to share the post.

Make a posting schedule and consider appointing someone to help develop posts and keep the church limber but missional using social media.

21. Form groups

Groups are key to *Rebuilding In-Person Worship*. Pursue groups for reaching benchmarks.

1. Definition of a group: a small gathering of people who want to do something together that connects them to your church and to Christianity.
2. Group types.

    - Study. You could read a book, do a Bible study, or study a topic of some kind.
    - Serving. The group serves either in the church or outside of it, in the neighborhood.*
    - Social. The group connects over an area of affinity, like sports or cooking.
    - Hybrid. Most groups seem to combine two or all-of-the-above categories.

What groups provide:

Opportunities for members and guests to:

- build relationships,
- practice faith,
- create belonging,
- involve non-believers,
- cultivate leadership, and
- fulfill God's mission.

How to initialize a group. There are two main ways:

1. Find a leader who has a skill or interest who can gather people
2. Connect people through interests on your contact list (phase 2, entry #14).

    - How to structure a group for growth. Most churches have long-standing groups that few new people would want to be involved in. Only in rare cases does a new person seamlessly fit into a group that has become established and long-standing. Yet when churches begin to get on the bandwagon for groups, the first thing they do is gather members. They expect to "attract" new people because the group is so relevant, in their eyes. You'll have to get past this institutional approach to group development when you pursue groups for your launch, when you do the following.

3. Start a new group with a new leader. Don't list existing groups as options.
4. Structure the new group with an equal number of members to new people.
5. Allow the group to bond, which they will.
6. Start a new group with a new leader if more people want to be involved in what the group stands for (study, serving, social, hybrid).
7. How to develop group content.

    a. Look for clues from the mission field. Who is your target and what are their interests?

    b. Invite. If the topic aligns with the mission field, it could, in fact, be somewhat appealing. However, you will still receive the most participation through invitations, specifically when a member of the launch team invites their plus-one to join the group.

    c. Lifestyle. Groups that hit the mark are often about things people struggle with. Mocktails and mixology could be a connecting point for Dry January participants. Geriatric parenting might be for seniors raising grandkids. Bibles, beets, and other delectables might be about foods you find in the Bible that are still relevant today—lots of diversity and opportunity for Bible discussion in group three.

8. Pay a leader. Hire a mixologist for lifestyle group one, a psychologist for lifestyle group two, or a Christian chef for lifestyle group three.

    a. Develop a sermon series. You won't be running multiple groups simultaneously as you launch, and your numbers are relatively small at this stage. Precede the start of the group with a sermon series about the topic of the group for encouragement to participate in the group. Or run the series simultaneously as the group meets.

    b. Hire staff, or not. It's common for churches to struggle with understanding group development, and even for larger churches with attendance of up to 250, to lack sufficient groups within their congregation. That's a mistake because you'll likely develop a lot of constituents who think of your church as their church, even if they don't participate during in-person worship—yet! You can hire staff to develop groups, but often leaders do that because they think it's easier. The launch team leader might be the one to develop groups. That won't cost you anything extra. If you do hire, be sure your person understands outreach, faith sharing, F.R.A.N.C., and the content of this entry.

    c. Digital platform. Find one that suits your church to stay organized with groups (and a lot of other things in your church).[1]

The Serving Groups of Worship Arts

Don't underestimate the value of entry points for people in serving in the church, primarily through the worship arts. The worship leader will have a significant influence on the formation of worship teams and communities. Consider the following ideas.

1. Singers
2. Band
3. Technology
4. Design

Additional commentary on serving in the worship arts:

- Know church values. If the primary worship leader is a serious Christ follower, does everyone else who sings before the congregation need to be?
- Pay some, not others. Some churches pay instrumentalists, such as a lead guitarist or a drummer. You can pay all instrumentalists, therefore, but you don't have to. Set your structure and allow the community to adjust.
- Technology is a key entry point. Some clients have found great success engaging youth in tech. New people will serve there as well, somewhat readily. Either way, you still need an adult organizer who organizes and trains volunteers. This could be a paid position.

- Worship design doesn't have to be a team. Organize your design group like a community, like the sermon prep community. You'll engage more people and generate more ideas if you don't require them to attend every meeting.

How will you organize your worship arts area, and who should help organize it?

22. Use (further develop) the online faith community!

The online faith community is a group, and not a small group. It's a growing group that may eventually yield subgroups due to its size. You might need to develop it with additional leaders. Much is available online in short teaching videos on organizing online groups. Initially, the launch team leader typically develops this group. Consider starter discussion questions:

- When do I feel fearful or frustrated while sharing faith?
- What's the impact of prayer on my outreach efforts?
- What is God teaching me about the mission field?
- What is God teaching me about myself?
- What are some threads of consistency from conversation to conversation?
- What do I need prayer for when I'm pursuing God beyond church walls?
- What does the mission field need prayer for?
- What areas of outreach do I need to brush up on or need more equipping for?
- What is my next step?

Write some short text posts. Plan for image posts and videos.

23. Plan-host three different-sized events

The launch process features three types of events.

- Plus-ones are mini events. You'll do most of those because everyone on the launch team conducts multiple mini-events with the person they're discipling. You will truly get the most bang for your buck with mini events. See entry #20.
- Mid-sized events. These are for about eight to twenty people. These are most important for developing groups because you can connect with new people, as well as other members and leaders. You need some mid-sized gatherings to reach critical mass.
- Large-scale events. These are over one hundred to well over one hundred. Significant events are very helpful for gaining recognition in your area, which is essential for a successful launch. However, they're challenging to develop, and they rarely translate into immediate new people coming to your church. You'll do the fewest of these for best results.

This entry focuses on mid-sized and large-scale events.

I. Mid-Sized Events

Mid-sized gatherings typically consist of eight to twenty people. A member has a plus-one they're discipling, and the member brings the plus-one to the mid-sized gathering with other members who are bringing their own plus-ones. There are equal numbers of members and guests.

A church I once coached had a member who was studying to be a sommelier. Some of the members had formed a wine-tasting group with her. After the training on outreach, they began working on ways to engage their non-churched friends into their group of about ten members. That wine-tasting group would become a plus-one social group of about twenty.

You could do the same type of thing without the vino if you wanted to—or with the vino, depending on your values—by having a family BBQ, for example. It would be in a member's backyard. Launch team participants would invite their plus-ones, as well as the plus-ones' partners or families. The balance of members to guests might not be exactly plus-one, due to the inclusion of families and significant relationships, but it would be close.

A backyard BBQ could be a one-time gathering. You could always repeat it, and in doing so, it can become a regular occurrence, with new people or some of the same individuals.

1. Organizing Mid-Sized Gatherings (Creating Ambience)

    - Make connections. Those who are trained in faith sharing can be connectors. Retrain the launch team at a launch team gathering.
    - Don't leave guests unattended. Even with plus-ones, church members can gravitate toward one another. Avoid member grouping when the member:
        - picks up the guest and drives the guest to the event,
        - introduces the guests around and connects guests with other guests over affinities,
        - makes sure the guest has something to drink and eat, or
        - provides food for the guests if it's a potluck.

2. Invitation

    - Save the date. Members send that to their guests ahead of time.
    - Say what it will be. Offer BBQ for church members and their non-church friends.
    - Use a digital invitation platform. You'll see who is on the invite list.
    - Say what you'll eat. Supply food options with great outdoor cooks.
    - Say what you'll do. Have plenty of games for kids and their families.

3. The actual gathering

    - Play background music. Invest in a Bluetooth device that you can bring from BBQ to BBQ.
    - Identify hosts. They are at the door to greet members and guests as they enter.
    - Have an icebreaker game or two for adults. This could be something that lets you mill around and talk to people while playing the game.
    - Time for the meal. Serve the meal not too quick, not too late, after people get there.
    - Have apps. Have chips, dips, and finger food ready to go as people enter.
    - Have a focal point. The launch team leader can speak for less than five minutes during dessert. People will disperse right after.

- Exchange. Remind guests to exchange contact information and to share it with the church.
- Dismissal. A host or two stands at the door and bids farewell!

4. Other organizational suggestions.

- Play stations. Offer this for kids and their families.
- Childcare. Pay day care workers more than their salary to help.
- Food prep. Members bring their own meat or a vegetarian/vegan option for themselves and their guests, for the chefs to grill.
- Eat together. Members and guests can eat together in groups of four to six-ish.

5. Follow up. All members follow up with their plus-one in a few days by email, text, or personal conversation.

6. Mid-sized event schedule.

- One mid-sized event per month or every six weeks from now until launch.
- Different people do different things with different groups.

7. Plan. Send invites about four weeks before the event.

Make additional notes about what you read, applying it to your setting.

II. Large-scale events

1. Large-scale events conceptually.
   Return to part I, chapter 5, to read an opening coaching story called "Capture Rate." Then go to part I, chapter 6 to read the story "Redefining Boundaries." Both of those coaching stories depict large-scale events.
   You need one to two significant events in a nine-to-eighteen-month launch sequence. Schedule one four weeks out from launch. If you have capacity for another, schedule it about two months before launch.

2. Organizing large-scale events. Don't put all your energy into a large-scale event!
   Church people love large-scale events because they see them as attractional. They are, which means you must work hard at pushing back against the attractional, institutional mindset. The countercultural approach for a large-scale event is to keep your focus on connecting people with Jesus and the church. That means members will intentionally interlope on another organization's event.

3. Interloping. Piggyback on something that is already happening in your area because it takes much less time to develop your role (e.g., a Fourth of July parade).

4. Lead time. Local rules apply! Inquire about the registration deadline for your participation.

5. Prep time. How long will it take to develop your participation? (e.g., building a float).

6. Engage the church. Who can help, even if not on the launch team?

7. Develop connectors—members, who:

    - pray about their role,
    - ask God to open the door to faith talk,
    - engage random people in small talk, or
    - are willing to ask for contact information.

8. Recruit connectors.

9. Engage all launch team members in your large-scale event—who will invite their people to it?

Note your own additional thoughts about large-scale events and the calendar for when to develop them organizationally. Who can get the ball rolling?

24. Revisit in-person worship

Resources on improving in-person worship dynamically can be found in part I, chapter 2. They include paying attention to size, flow, prayer, and sermon-prep processes. The recommendation was to start making worship changes to in-person worship in part I by addressing these areas before ever considering changing style.

This is the time to assess your progress. How is in-person worship going? Are you ready to apply more direct development to in-person worship? Keeping focused on worship quality is always essential. What seems to be good quality now can change as you add new people; calendar when you'll review worship quality and with whom.

What else needs to happen to support in-person worship? Any come-to-Jesus conversations required? Make notes and a calendar.

25. Launch-team gatheringIt's perhaps six to eight weeks since your first launch team gathering. Repeat the first launch team agenda.

- Add in training. At the meeting, include training for mid-sized events and group development. Briefly discuss worship changes without going into too much detail.
- See entry #24 for developing your training on mid-sized events. See entry #22 for a refresher on group development. See the previous entry for insights into what to say about worship in your church.

What are you seeing that's characterizing your launch team right now? Are they joyful, stressed, depressed, or hopeful? What type of encouragement do they need? What additional training will help them progress? Include those things in your next gathering.

26. Hire a worship leader

If you're starting an entirely new service, you may be in the position of hiring a worship leader. That's harder than you think. The biggest problem: churches don't pay enough. The churches that pay well draw better-quality musical leaders to your candidate pool.

Most churches are fighting the old institutionalism of valuing one kind of worship and one type of music. Many churches still don't grasp that the quality of the music is the most critical factor, not style. If you're going to produce a modern service, you need a contemporary worship leader who you pay enough to warrant their devotion to creating a high-quality experience. The following job description outlines all the factors to consider when finding a good candidate.

A. Advertising

Understand and communicate primary duties. The worship leader:

1. plans music;

2. practices music personally and with the worship team;

3. grows the worship team, including the tech area (at this stage. As you grow, tech and music might separate.);

4. sometimes is involved in worship planning: It is not always necessary for the worship leader to be directly involved in worship planning for the entire service. Often, your worship leader will have a day job. Only much larger churches can afford a full-time worship leader with benefits. Cut number 4 if you need to cut something to make the job appealing for your candidate.

B. Entry Point

The worship team is a place where new people will land. It's a serving area for those called and gifted to up front worship leadership and technology. Leadership skills for a worship leader that help engage new people in worship arts are the following.

- Plays a lead instrument: Could be. But not required.
- Builds teams and groups: Critical.
- Finds lead musicians if they don't play a lead instrument? 100 percent
- Is a lead vocalist? Could be. But not required.
- Finds a lead vocalist if they can't fulfill that calling? Yes.
- Matches the mission field. Has to.
- Knows the music the mission field connects to? Without a doubt.
- Willing to participate in social media? Absolutely.
- Builds teams and groups. At the top of the list.

C. Salary

Many great candidates will have day jobs. It's better to find a quality candidate with a day job and pay a salary for ¼ to ½ time than to pay an hourly rate.

Pay is local. There's not one right salary nationwide that defines a good package for a quality worship leader. Follow this process that one of my clients used, and now I tell everyone about it:

- Ask growing churches in your area what they pay, in order to see what the going rate is.
- Cut the figure in half for half-time, in fourths for ¼ time.
- Add $1,000 or $2,000 to the ¼-time figure.
- Add $3,000 to the ⅓-time figure.
- Add $5,000 to the half-time figure.

D. Where to Find Quality Candidates

- Start in your church. Is there a candidate who fits the profile of a great candidate? If so, or if not, continue to produce a great talent pool:
- Post on Craig'slist, Indeed, and denominational publications. This will produce moderate results.
- Reach out to very large churches. Talk with the worship director, not the senior pastor. See if there is someone in their midst whom they're grooming for worship leadership. This could be the most important thing you do.
- Put up a flyer. Sometimes there are factories or coffee shops or gyms or gas stations or any other place where people (your mission field) hang out or work who might have a person ready to be called to a part-time gig like this. Don't leave any stone unturned.
- Remember the U. Many churches are in proximity to colleges. Put fliers there and post in their publications if you can.
- Ask members. Don't short-shrift people already in seats! They might know someone.

E. Exit Strategy

- Tell your hire that you're hiring for a season to see if it's a good fit. Everyone will know quickly whether it is or isn't. If you misjudged the fit or if your candidate was not truthful about who they are and their capabilities, it won't be good for them or your church to stick around.

  If it is a good fit, then build in a salary bump at the six-month point. You can put that in the advertising to find the candidate.

Make an initial pass at writing your worship leader job description.

27. Revisit in-person worship—again.

Have you hired a worship leader? She or he needs to be involved in a discussion about your worship flow and some content. Prepare all hearts and minds for this input in advance. 

28. Adjust Calendar

What sticky notes do you need to move around?

Phase Three Postscript

Somewhere in here is where it usually hits for churches that have taken on the journey to share faith beyond church walls: you want to quit! I said it would happen! You wish it weren't taking so much time. You want to have a life. Everyone is rubbing you the wrong way. The staff member is whiny. The launch team participant is anxious. The names you're adding to your contact list are not that many.

Have you contacted your intercessors recently? Have you developed in-person worship so that there's a chance to confess your worries before God in the presence of community? Have you streamlined your schedule? Are you praying daily for the launch team, for new people, for your F.R.A.N.C. list?

Just thought I'd ask.

Phase Four

RAMP UP

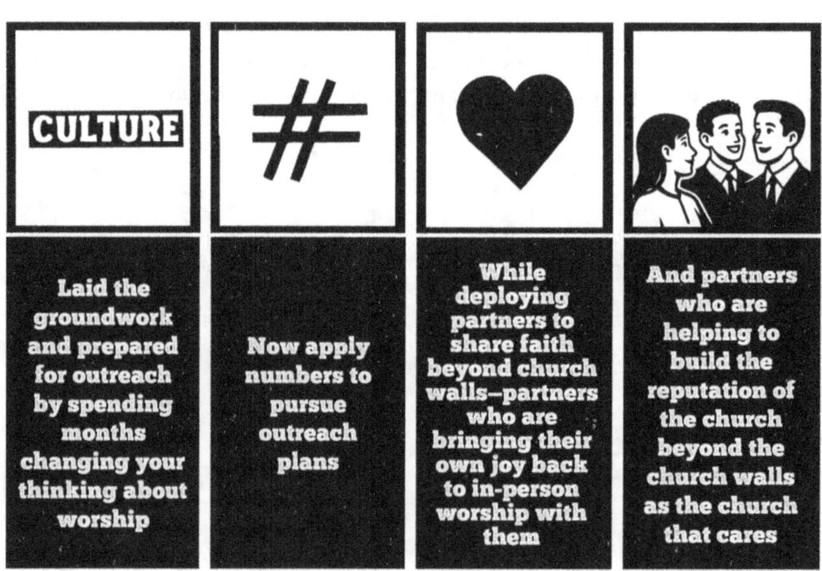

Phase Four Notes

You're ramping up to launch. You've been building momentum for several months. Perhaps you've already seen some bump-ups in worship in your building and in community connections. People are starting to hear about you beyond the church walls. You have more names on your contact list than those you know personally. Members are getting excited because they're seeing fruit.

Plan some to-dos to increase your visibility. Be bold. Be strong. Be courageous, for the Lord your God is with you everywhere you go.

29. Calendar—personalize and read ahead.

Produce another large chart for your wall!

30. Update in-person worship (with spiritual practices)

I've shared faith with an atheist on an airplane, a new-age clothing store supervisor who was the granddaughter of a Christian church planter, and the son of a close friend. All of them were in their twenties. I found a common thread: spiritual practices. The atheist was into solitude. The store manager loved studying, though it was of numerology and angel sightings, not so much the Bible! The son of the friend valued community through gaming.

Christianity is a disciplined way of life. We pursue solitude, study, community, and other practices for spiritual growth. People of any age can seek a faith discipline on their own or with a mentor's help. A mentor is a worship leader. The value of worship leading is foundational to *Rebuilding In-Person Worship.* It was an entire chapter in part I (chapter 2).

Where Are You in Your Journey to Rebuild In-person Worship?

Adding a focus on spiritual practices and disciplines to worship would further strengthen the community's worship. Worship itself is a spiritual discipline. So is listening to God's word. You can deepen the worship experience and help participants meet God in community by pursuing those practices.

This entry was not included in part I because so many smaller congregations with worship attendance under 250 still struggle with control over worship in their buildings. The way into worship changes for most churches is through prayer, sermon preparation, and focus on worship dynamics (part I). Now that you've begun to pursue faith sharing, or maybe before if you're reading ahead, you can add in a new focus on spiritual practices during worship.

Uplifting spiritual practices during the public gathering will build worship dynamics. And if you're trying to engage new people in public, in-person worship, increasing worship leadership through spiritual practices will remind them of the ways they pursue self-discovery through various disciplines and faith practices already in their own lives. It's just that now they're pursuing those practices to meet God too.

Phase Four: Ramp Up

29. Calendar - personalize and read ahead
30. Update /in-person worship
31. Do demos I
32. Do demos II
33. Do service
34. Do media blitz
35. Do reality check
36. Adjust Calendar

Increase prayer
Share faith

1-2 months

A New Aspect of Faith-talk to Add to Your Personal Outreach Plan

When ramping up toward launch and meeting new people in the community, you will find some who will want to know what your church's in-person gathering is like. You can tell them it's spiritually based and incorporates ways to meet with God that they might already be familiar with. Now that's a conversation starter.

1. Spiritual practices you already include in the public service

The outline below follows the five parts of the worship service introduced in the worship comparison charts in chapter 2, part I.

a. Gathering. The spiritual practice is community.

b. Praise. The spiritual practice is praise in community.

c. Proclamation. The spiritual practice is hearing God's word.

d. Prayer. The spiritual practice is confession.

e. Dismissal. The spiritual practice is evangelism.

2. Building spiritual practices during in-person worship

   a. Gathering and building community.

      i. Focus on the slideshow/announcement reel. Show slides of the church in mission with groups of people working together.

      ii. Repeat some slides during the welcome and announcement segment, commenting on how they illustrate people working together.

   b. Praise. The spiritual practice is praise in community.

      i. After the praise segment, the person speaking to the congregation to welcome them can mention that praise is a discipline of the faith that brings you closer to God. You can reinforce the idea of discipline when you pray, tying the praise segment to the welcome and announcements.

      ii. If you share a testimonial video right after the praise segment and before the welcome and announcements, bring up the spiritual practice of faith sharing as a value of your faith community.

      iii. If you use creeds, invite new people not to participate in confessing their faith if they're not ready. Invite them to join if they want to see what it feels like to say something confessional out loud, and to see what God does with that in their spirit when they do.

   c. Proclamation. The spiritual practice is hearing God's word.

      i. If you read scripture before or during the message, remind worshipers that listening to the word of God is a spiritual practice that is often best absorbed when repeated. If you keep the passage short, you can read it aloud, then have the community read it with you.

      ii. Include silence either before or after the passage. Begin the silence with a prayer for people to hear God. You can be silent for up to one minute. Keep track of the time on your watch or phone while simultaneously interceding for the community during the silence. You can tell them you have been interceding on their behalf.

      iii. Remind people that they're engaging in deep learning time, with connections to the Bible. Provide scripture passages for people to study on their own. You can create note sheets for people to follow along with the message. Lift that up as part of the discipline of study.

      iv. Consider a sermon series on spiritual practices, perhaps annually.

      v. Tie a sermon series on spiritual practices to group development. While you'll have different groups that often follow their own agenda, it's not wrong to sometimes ask all groups to participate in a common agenda. You can try fasting, solitude, or silence.

d. Prayer. The spiritual practice is confession.

i. A lot was said about the interactive, confessional prayer after the message in part I, chapter 2. The prayer sequence is to pray for myself, then someone I know, then someone I don't know. You're introducing the spiritual practice of intercession along with personal confession. Remind people that they're interceding. 

e. Dismissal. The spiritual practice is evangelism.

i. As part of your dismissal or benediction, remind people that they're witnesses to faith when they leave the building. Ask them to pray to be able to tell others about faith and their own faith story.

ii. Teach about faith sharing and rebuilding in-person worship annually, and how focusing on spiritual practices increases worship.

3. Worship leading
Any up-front worship leader can help direct a congregation during worship by adding language about (in this case) spiritual practices. You're helping participants focus on their own experience of God as they intentionally pursue God through faith.

4. Worship changes
Adding new language about spiritual practices during worship is a change. Is there anyone you need to talk to for inclusion, even if only to say you're going in a deeper direction during worship? The conversation alone will deepen worship.

a. Fasting during in-person worship: Fasting heightens your senses to God's input. You can fast from food, TV, cussing—what's your vice? God is going to speak to you in new ways because of your deficit.

b. You can fast during public worship too, as a body. What is the most revered part of the service? Eliminate it for a season, then coach the congregation to listen anew to God about possessiveness, loss, and other insights they gain through the experience.

Joys and Concerns, Children's Message

Two areas of worship that seem sacred but are not always impactful for more than a few people are reflected in this entry heading. Fasting from them for a season would be a spiritually focused way to consider eliminating them, if you aren't using fasting manipulatively. 

What are initial thoughts on increasing spiritual practices during in-person worship? 

31. Do demos: One

Demos refer to music and performance in the secular culture by a worship leader to engage with new people with the church's style. Do one or more demos a month during this season.

1. The modern music demo

a. Who does it:

i. The worship leader: a one-person show using electronics and loops

ii. The entire band or just a couple of people

b. Include:
    i. Secular music and sacred music
    ii. Some spoken commentaries and "working the crowd"
    iii. Business cards
    iv. A pitch for participation in the group
    v. Personal connections with the crowd between sets
c. Demo opportunities could be:
    i. Open mic night at a bar
    ii. Music in the park. Check to see if you need any kind of public performance permit.
    iii. Posting videos of gatherings. Be sure you have someone taking videos!
d. Invite the launch team and connectors to demos
    i. Provide invitation tools
    ii. Gather contact information when possible

2. The traditional music demo
    a. Who does it
        i. The choir
        ii. An ensemble
    b. Include:
        i. Hymns
        ii. Choir praise music
        iii. Maybe a secular song for a choir
        iv. Some spoken commentaries and "working the crowd"
        v. Business cards
        vi. A pitch for participation in the group
        vii. Personal connections with the crowd between sets
        viii. Posting videos online
    c. Demo options
        i. Music in the park
        ii. Open mic night
    d. Include launch team members and connectors: same as above
    e. Why stop now? Find your sweet spot and develop your rhythm for doing more demos even after your launch.

How will you develop demos?

32. Do demos: Two

If you've developed an entirely new worship format, you may need to build in some practice time for mastering it. Consider:

1. Space dynamics: The right space for the correct critical mass number for your launch
2. Flow dynamics: A worship service that engages and doesn't distract
3. Worship times: A time that suits your mission field. You might experiment with different times during your demos.
4. Worship leading up front: You've worked as a worship leader in the community, and up-front leaders understand their role.
5. Preaching topics: You've worked with a sermon prep community, and you're lined up in advance.
    a. Demo topics might be less formal and more geared to continuing to build the launch team and outreach.
6. Prayer themes: You would still do interactive, confessional prayer as part of your worship flow.
7. Technology and glitching: You have a tech leader, and that leader has developed a tech community.
    a. Various participants from the tech community are attending the demo to identify and fix glitches.
8. Set up and tear down: This is a significant factor in the demo if you're in a temporary space or in a storefront.
    a. You need a leader and a community to set up and tear down weekly. They should all be present at the demos to work out the kinks.
9. Who participates: Invite the launch team personally.
    a. The launch team can invite their person from the F.R.A.N.C. list.
    b. No formal advertising beyond that.
10. How many times: You have one to two months for this phase.
    a. Are you ready in one month, or do you need two?

You could do a demo per week. How many do you need?

Do you need some worship demos before launch? Who will develop and schedule them?

33. Do service: Ministry with, ministry to

"Acts of service" is a hands-on way to engage new people, both those you serve and those who do the act of service with you. There's a distinction between the two categories, and it affects adding new people to your contact list (which, in turn, affects benchmarks and reaching critical mass).

Most churches I've worked with that value serving the poor rarely have anyone in their church who is poor. Economics is a great divider in developing a faith community. Significantly few leaders can bridge the economic disparity gap. There is nothing wrong with that leader. It's just how God wired you. Distinguishing between "ministry with" and "ministry to" is essential for understanding that reality.

Ministry With

These are the people with whom you have affinity and who will do ministry with you. They will do "ministry to" with you. See #2, below.

Ministry To

This is the work the church does to serve those who won't come to your church but can benefit from its ministries. Often, those the church serves are at a different economic status than your faith community. If you were to invite them and they came but saw many cars in the parking lot that symbolize wealth, they wouldn't join you in worship, no matter how hard you tried. If you attempt to develop a group with or for those who don't fit your church's demographic, it can come off as arrogant and inauthentic. It's not impossible to start such a group with the right leader and heart. But it still will be challenging to blend in those who struggle economically with those who don't, in most cases.

Doing Acts of Service with Care: Hands-on Ministry

Hands-on ministry is different than just giving money. Develop a ministry with a hands-on approach. Teach faith sharing!

1. How to organize ministry to
    a. Do what's local and sometimes immediate (see examples, below).
    b. Staff service projects with connectors.
    c. Provide invite tools and ways for recipients to get in touch with you if they want.
    d. Be prepared to capture contact information.
    e. Take videos mostly of those who are doing the ministry with whom you're doing ministry, not those who are receiving the ministry. The latter could be invasive.
    f. Post pics on social media and use them in an announcement reel during worship gathering times.
2. Examples of local acts of service
    a. Paying for everyone's laundry in the Laundromat (in a college town)
    b. Shoveling out fire hydrants from a blizzard (in a northern climate)
    c. Paying for everyone's coffee at the drive-thru line (where coffee shops are popular)
    d. Covering students' lunches at the local college for a day (if that's your mission field)
    e. Bringing meals to homeless teens (teenage homelessness is a growing phenomenon)
    f. Cleaning up various neighborhoods after a storm (could happen anywhere)!
3. How to develop ministry with to pursue ministry to
    a. The value is to engage new people in ministry who will be doing ministry with you.
    b. The launch team should reach out person-to-person with their F.R.A.N.C. list person to invite them to participate.
    c. Post invites also on social media.
    d. Use RSVP so that you have a good idea of who will be there.

4. How many acts of service do you need? Generally, acts of service are low-key. They do require organization, but not large groups of people.
    a. Appoint an organizer: The appointee is on your launch team or is a congregation member or staff member who isn't on the launch team but values what you're doing and has organizational gifts.
    b. Develop different events for different configurations of launch team participants and their guests, and post the schedule.
5. Why stop now?
    a. Acts of service can define a church as much as music. Keep doing them and pursue outreach with them, which means hands-on, faith sharing.

Which acts of service do you think will impact your territory beyond the church? How will you engage persons on your contact list to participate in them? How can you reinforce those acts of service with group development and messaging?

34. Do media blitz

1. What's a media blitz?
    a. An organized ad campaign that's timed to begin toward the end of this phase of your step-up chart and continue through launch season (the next column) and right up to your launch date.
2. Media blitz resources include:
    a. Fliers, emails, and possibly snail mail
    b. Snail mail works in some areas. You'll have to find out about yours. If you do it, your numbers should be very large, as you'll only get about ½ to 1 percent of the entire batch that will come to your church.
    c. There is a financial cost for snail mail advertising that can be worth it if your numbers are large enough.
3. Details to include in your media blitz
    a. Launch dates and themes
    b. Featured speakers and activities
    c. Why you are launching
    d. Who you are
4. The role of launch team participants
    a. They media-blitz their own people, they're discipling, and according to a pre-arranged schedule that the leadership provides them
    b. They need advertising support in the form of how many times to send their notices and when, and maybe how to effectively use the social media or email platform they're using
5. Organization team
    a. Someone who knows about advertising or who can learn and develop a team

Who will develop your media blitz? What information do they need to tie everything together? What's the timeline?

35. Do reality check

A reality check is numerical. Are you where you should be numerically in your launch process? What are the implications if you're not? Below is your reality check checklist. Have you/we:

- diligently increased worship dynamics as narrated in part I;
- taken the time we needed to pursue the step-up columns for part II ;
- been in touch with personal intercessors along the way;
- spent a lot of time pursuing our personal outreach plans (the whole launch team);
- scrupulously added names to a growing contact list;
- recorded enough names so that the contact list is close to 10 × the number we need to reach critical mass;
- reached about ⅓ the number of critical mass, growing the launch team;
- generally felt a buzz both in the church and beyond it as the community has come to know us as a serious, faith-sharing church; and
- understood exactly where we are and are confident that we can reach our numbers in the next few weeks?

1. If you can say yes to all of the above, you're on track for launch, even if it might not feel like it.
2. If you cannot say yes to all of the above, you may need to regroup.
    a. Regrouping options when you're not going to reach critical mass:
        i. Launch anyway, even if you're not where you should be numerically.
            1. If you don't reach critical mass numbers and you launch anyway, your worship gathering will most likely languish. If your launch is a relaunch, languishing may be more of the same. That can be disheartening for those who believed you would succeed. Pushing back your launch might be the better option.
        ii. Launch anyway if you're willing to repeat the launch process soon.
            1. It's possible to launch even without critical mass if you discern it's appropriate to repeat your launch process in a few months. Repeating the launch process is key. It works when you notice some energy beyond the church walls for your church. You have increased your church's reputation, but you haven't been as diligent about inviting new people to cross the line from lurking to participating.
        iii. Push the launch date back.
            1. Churches can fear doing this, but it's not wrong or necessarily harmful. It will require hunkering down with your launch team and looking at how many more numbers you need to reach critical mass. Then ask yourself, How long will it take us to get to that number? Reset your launch date accordingly.

iv. Don't fear the unsettledness either way.

1. Most new people don't pay that much attention to the dates of your launch until they've seen the dates a few times, and it's closer to your launch. If you haven't done a tremendous amount of advertising yet, you're not in danger of creating whiplash by changing the dates. It will be unsettling for your launch team, but you can turn that into a worship dynamic through prayer and building trust.

v. Launching a few times: for the tiny church (under thirty in worship)

1. I've worked with some small churches that have pursued launching a new service but have had trouble reaching critical mass, even though they've done nearly everything right. Small, aging churches sometimes must launch a couple of times to get to where they want to go.

Caveat: don't pursue multiple launches off the bat. Wait to see where you are in the launch process, even when starting with a tiny constituency. Consider the sequence below only when you get to this part of the process and you're concerned that you're not on track numerically

3. How to develop multiple launches within a few months
   a. Be clear about critical mass.
   b. Study your contact list to increase it.
   c. Regroup on personal outreach plans (part I-, chapter 5; and part II-, entry #19).
   d. Pursue space dynamics and create artistic, portable banners to help shrink the room.
   e. Pursue all worship dynamics during in-person worship.
   f. Launch on your date to give numbers a small boost as a "soft launch."
   g. Strategically plan another launch within three to six months.
   h. Clue in the launch team and take the temperature. Can you do it?
   i. Build in rest between launches.
   j. Celebrate: Don't forget what you've accomplished, even if you must launch again within a few months.

Be clear and truthful: How on track are you and what's next? 

36. Adjust calendar

Whether you're pushing back your launch date or launching on time but launching again in a few months, it's going to impact your calendar with items that might not be represented in the step-up column you're currently in. Use the two examples below to help you visualize.

Launch One: Reach 1/2 of critical mass

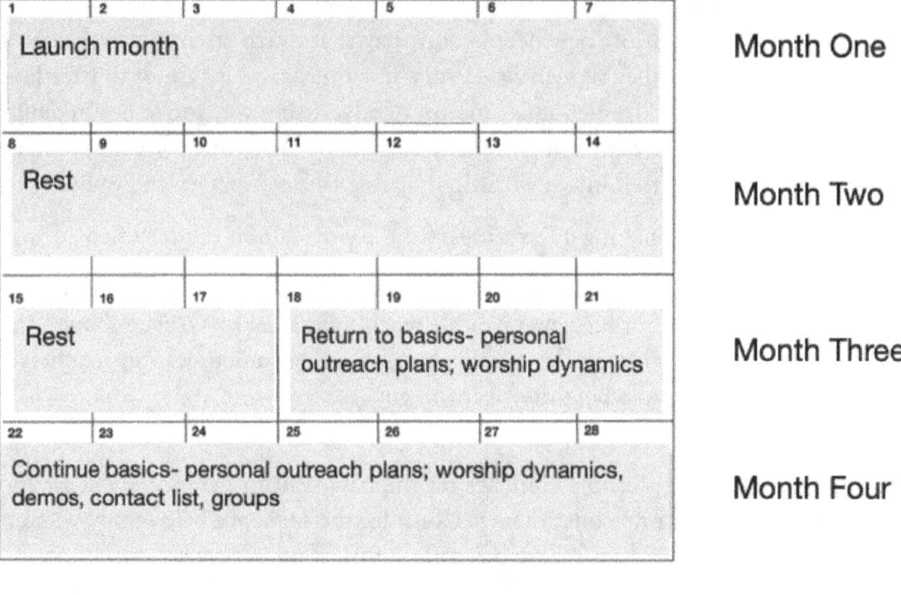

Launch Two: Reach critical mass

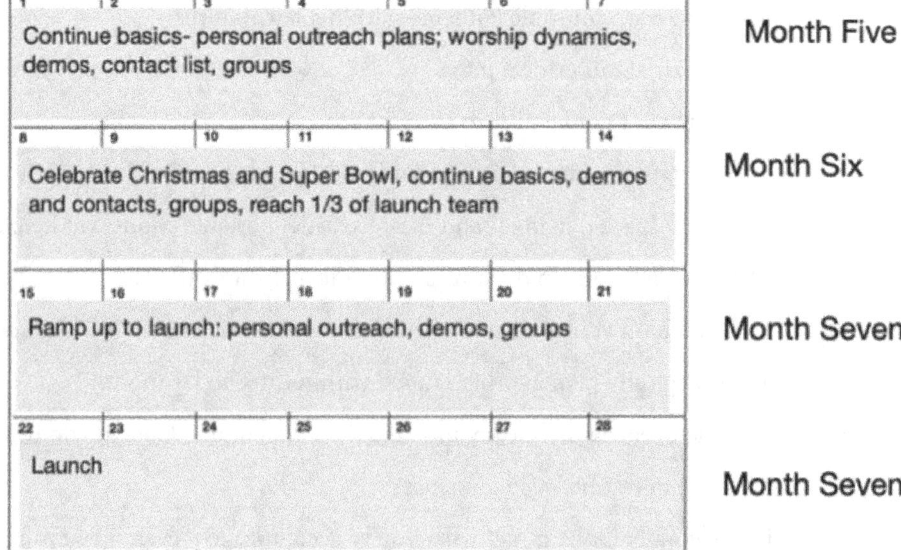

What to Notice in the Two Charts

If you delay your launch or do multiple launches a few months apart, you'll experience a lot of emotions. Emotions are part of worship development. Through prayer and spiritual practices, you can continue to build in-person worship despite your setbacks. Use all of this to build trust. God is still with you.

Phase Five

LAUNCH

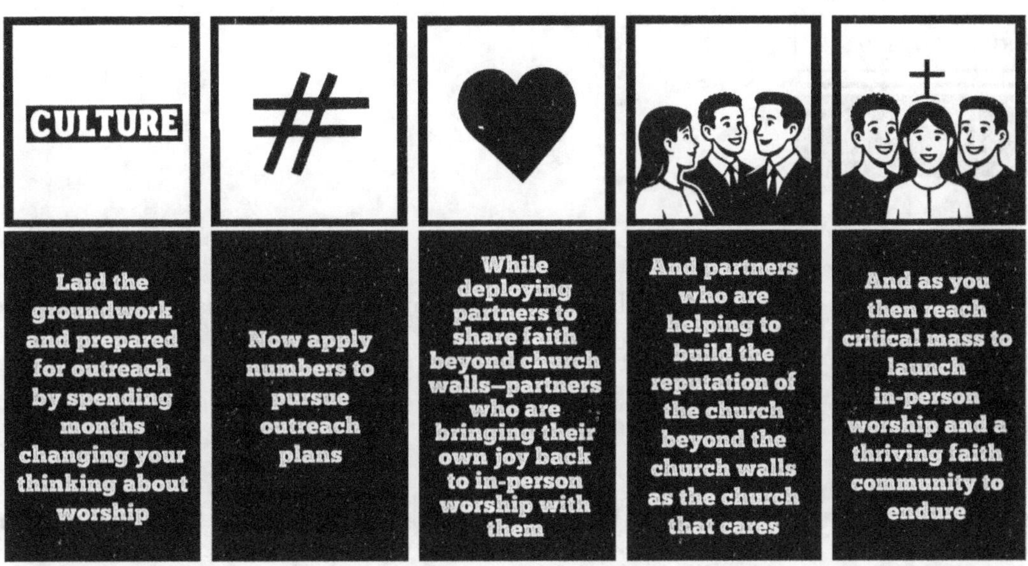

Phase Five Notes

Your stomach is in knots. You're losing sleep. Your lists have lists. You've checked them twice (× twice). You're pretty sure you're where you're supposed to be, but you never know. You must triple your launch team numbers, which have already tripled since you started, and your contact list has 10 × the number of names you need for critical mass. Still, your palms are sweating, and you know there are no guarantees.

You have something to confess! Confession is worship! Worship is surrender! That's how to approach this phase.

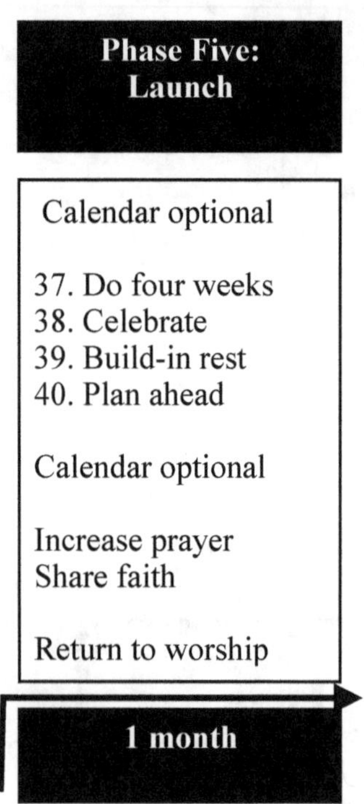

Because all calendaring has been completed to get you to launch, you may choose not to calendar during this season. Calendar as needed to stay on track.

37. Do four weeks

The chart below lays out a four-week plan for different times of the year for launching, with a serving theme as an example. Develop your own theme.

Serving theme

Week	Fall launch	Winter launch	Spring launch	Guest speaker
One	Bless backpacks	Bless skis-sleds	Bless wheels	School principal
Two	Make food	Provide clothing	Provide cells	Shelter director
Three	Supply groceries	Supply groceries	Supply groceries	Fire chief
Four	Raise funds	Raise funds	Raise funds	Sports coach

Explaining the chart:

1. The blessings of week one

    - The focus is on the local school and relationships you've developed with the school as part of your outreach and faith sharing.
    - The connection with the school principal could be that you shared faith with him or her, or that they love what you do.

2. Serving at the homeless shelter

    - You might set up space for worshipers to make sandwiches on their way out of worship, then bring them to the homeless shelter.
    - Worshipers saw on your media blitz that they should bring clothes to worship.
    - If teen homelessness is a thing in your area, donate cell phones for kids to stay in touch with their case workers.
    - The homeless shelter director has become a friend during your launch sequence.

3. Connecting with the fire chief

    - An option for developing worship themes for launch is to repeat what you do each week. Bringing groceries each week represents repetition.
    - Groceries can be for victims of fires and for the firefighters.
    - The fire chief, perhaps, was already a Christian and invited you to go on fire runs with the firehouse.

4. Sports and schools

    - Some communities are very focused on sports and sponsorships for high school and grade school kids. If that's your community, make the most of it. Please get to know the athletic coach and have them speak at your launch. If the coach wants to bring a kid to speak, that's awesome!
    - Help fund the teams and athleticism each week of your launch with a special fundraiser.

    a. Weekly worship order

        - Look at the worship flowcharts in part I, chapter 2. Where will guest speakers go?

What themes are you considering? Who might be your speakers? Who can help organize your launch themes and worship?

38. Celebrate

B.Y.O.J. (Bring Your Own Joy)! You've been faith sharing, and you've touched too many lives to count. The community beyond your church has heard about you. You have reached critical mass. You're launching! Wow! You're awesome! And God is so good . . . (*All* the time!!)

39. Build in rest

Four weeks of launch runs into four more weeks of church runs into four more months of church. You won't stop faith sharing. But you will stop launching until you do it again. See the next heading for when to launch again.

Right now, plan. Take a break from the pace of launching by simply enjoying all God has done. But do keep praying that God will use you to share faith. You have put a lot of systems in place to help new people land. They will if you keep adding names to your contact list, and then they get the memo. They won't get the memo if they're not on your list.

The systems you've built mean you get a break.

40. Plan ahead

At some point, you'll move on to part III of this material. It might be eighteen months to a couple of years. But if you want to continue impacting your neighborhood, you must go through another launch process—calendar when you're going to start looking ahead to part III—in about six months.

Part III

INSIDE AND OUTSIDE YOUR BUILDING

Phase Six

KEEP GOING

Phase Six Notes

In part II, you had five phases for launching.

- The first phase was what you did before you got to part II.
- You began changing behavior with phase 2.
- Launch was phase 5.
- There is one more phase of development: phase 6.
- You thought you were done.
- Au contraire.
- Read this phase with identity as you write your own ending.

The Third Act Break

If you've ever studied film, you know about the second act break: the point in the story at which the protagonist must live with their decisions and cannot go back.

We could call part III of *Rebuilding In-Person Worship* the third act break. Things have changed because of you pursuing part II. Now you're at the point of no return. Maybe you can see a lot of fruit and that's making you feel good about yourself. Fair enough! That buoyance could lull you into thinking that you did your part in faith sharing beyond the church walls and now you're done, because you have succeeded. Your church has turned things around, mostly. But here's the question: will the turnaround endure? Maybe for a while. But without a continued focus on outreach, you'll start to see the signs of stress and the cracks in the foundation. Maybe even within the next year. That's the beginning of the return to decline.

And that's nothing new. It's the current landscape of churches everywhere. They thrived. Then they didn't do any outreach, and now they have but a few members.

You're at a discernment crossroads. What will you do next?

While you're considering the answer to that question, take a gander down memory lane, as the hurdles you crossed and milestones you reached are why you're in your third act break!

Numerical Growth

Part of your growth has been numerical. If you were about 20 in worship attendance and you launched or relaunched worship, you could now be pushing 50 in worship. Look at you! Your next hurdle would be about 75 to 100. If you started at 100, you might have moved to about 150, so about 200 would be next. Now you're getting to the large-church stage. If you started at about 200 to 250, then you're moving into a very different category of church: the large or very large church, which used to be about 500 in worship. Now, churches of 250 to 350 are considered large, when they used to be mid-sized. Hit the pause button. Is that what you're really called to: continual numerical growth? Maybe not. But maybe. Numerical growth is a sign of fruit. And if you don't have an influx of new people to existing worship, it indicates decline.

But numerical growth opens the doorway to the need for learning new leadership behaviors. Every time you reach a new numerical benchmark, your leadership has to morph. If you can't shift, it may be time for another leader. With your experience, you can return to a faith community that's similar to the one you just grew when you started growing it. You can do it again. How does that thought impact you?

Structural Growth

If you have done the organizational and spiritual work outlined in this material, you likely have seen an influx of new people. To organize new people, you've put some new structures in place, including groups to support in-person worship. You've put together a sermon prep team, and you're getting direct input from the mission field. You've added more prayer to worship. You've added more prayer in your own life. Your worship flow has grown more engaging. You've grown clearer about your beliefs as a faith community, and you're not afraid to express them aloud in public worship. You've grown humbler about conflict yet more confident, surrendering to God and continuing to follow your mission. What if you were to go back to the way things were? Would all of those accomplishments endure?

Raising Up from Within Growth

So many mainline churches seem to ignore the idea that you'd raise up a leader from within the church, especially someone who looks spiritually immature right now. But maybe you see something in them. They're more than a volunteer. If you have pursued rebuilding in-person worship, then you might see that you've been raising up some leaders along the way since you have had to mentor them to hand things off to them. Your faith community will be stronger because you're raising up leaders from within. It's work to do that. Is the work worth it to you at this point?

Personal Spiritual Growth

Your most important growth has been spiritual. You've transformed as a Christ follower by learning to share faith beyond church walls, and as a leader by developing the systems to take others with you. Praise God, for real.

But has your church's culture entirely changed? Probably not yet. There's more to do for a new culture to take root fully. If your heart is now for the mission of the church and the mission field more than for maintenance, then you're in the right spot to go even further with culture change. . But you have to choose it. Are you ready for that?

Not a Program

What you have taken on in pursuing rebuilding in-person worship is not a program. It's a way of doing life personally and corporately, as a church. It involves systems and processes. Many of those are spelled out in this written material. And yet, most invitations to participate in this material throughout the workbook have encouraged you to develop your own insights and maybe your own way of doing things. If you're thinking about taking the steps to continue this work into the future, you can use this material again, and again. Every time you do it, it might look slightly different. What are you thinking about how to develop a system to repeat this work over time?

Age and Calling

This process has been demanding. And you might not want to do it again. Except, if you let it go now, a part of you will die, and so will your church. Following God into growth is always a demanding choice for a human. That choice might look different at different points in your ministry. If you're under thirty and grew up in the church, you may not have ever seen a model of personal outreach and faith sharing. This has been a new experience for you. How are you thinking about incorporating faith-sharing into your ministry work down the road? What do you want to accomplish? If you're between thirty and fifty, you're in that age range that churches love for leaders. That can create a lull in you because people like you for your age and energy. And faith-sharing, as the heartbeat of worship development, is demanding. You might prefer to be well-loved instead of taking the road less traveled for pursuing faith development. What's your inkling about that?

Somewhere between fifty and sixty-five, you'll start to think about what you've accomplished and your leadership legacy. You did well to launch or relaunch a service. Will you do it again before you retire? Will you create the systems to be sure others will take it on when you leave?

And then, some are closer to my age, which is past retirement. If you've never pursued faith development and talking with others about Jesus, it's not too late. God seems to keep using us. How do you continue to serve to further the God's realm even in your later years?

Laypersons Too

This is a leadership book. But laypersons are leaders, so don't think this material is only for the lead pastor. What do you want out of your life as a Christ follower? Can you interpret this time as your third-act break, not to quit but to continue serving by sharing your faith beyond church walls?

The local church will not endure unless non-ordained leaders are willing to take on the calling to share their faith beyond church walls, fulfilling their role as disciples who make disciples. Doing so increases in-person worship. Churches need thriving in-person worship to endure, because of the nature of worship as God's milieu. Whoever you are:

- pray,
- walk the parish,
- plan, and
- look at the final step-up chart.

The New Ending to Your Story

You've been working on rewriting the ending to your church's story. If your church is overcome by institutionalism, we already know the ending. And we didn't even have to read ahead.

When you begin to overcome institutionalism, the story's ending isn't ever finished. On that note, you can write your own outlines for Column 6, Phase 6 in the step-up chart.

Phase One: Lay Groundwork	**Phase Two: Form Launch**	**Phase Three: Share Faith**	**Phase Four: Ramp Up**	**Phase Five: Launch**	**Phase Six: Ongoing**
Step / task # 1 All Of Part One In *Rebuilding In-Person Worship*	2. Calendar - personalize & read ahead 3. Engage a coach 4. Confirm target 5. Set critical mass 6. Review the math 7. Match members 8. Set schedule-launch date 9. Plan gathering 10. Write descript.-A 11. Write descript.-B 12. Recruit the launch team 13. Design tools 14. List contacts 15. Host gathering 16. Begin outreach 17. Adjust calendar Increase prayer Share faith	18. Calendar - personalize and read ahead 19. Follow F.R.A.N.C. 20. Tap media 21. Form groups 22. Use online community 23. Plan-host events 24. Revisit in-person worship 25. Launch-team gathering 26. Hire worship leader 27. Revisit in-person worship - again 28. Adjust Calendar Increase prayer Share Faith	29. Calendar - personalize and read ahead 30. Update /in-person worship! 31. Do demos I 32. Do demos II 33. Do service 34. Do media blitz 35. Do reality check 36. Adjust Calendar Increase prayer Share faith	Calendar optional 37. Do four weeks 38. Celebrate 39. Build in rest 40. Plan ahead Calendar optional Increase prayer Share faith	41. Pray 42. Gather people 43. Teach worship and outreach 44. Walk-drive the parish 45. Develop and follow your plan Increase prayer Share faith
2 to 6 months	**2 to 4 months**	**3 to 5 months**	**1-2 months**	**1 month**	**New Timeline**

CULTURE
CULTURE

SOURCES

Chapter One: Discerning Your Role

1. Author-led group coaching is available for this material. For larger projects for churches approaching 200 in worship or more, individual coaching is an important consideration.

Chapter Two: Leading Worship

1. Martha Grace Reese, *Unbinding the Gospel: Real Life Evangelism* (Chalice Press: 2006).

2. Reese, *Unbinding the Gospel*, 5.

Chapter Five: Doing the Math

1. Carey Nieuwhof, host, *The Carey Nieuwhof Leadership Podcast*, podcast, episode 574, "Warren Bird and JJ Vasquez on The New Math of Church Plants, How Church Planting Is Changing and What Happens When Superman Dies," May 30, 2023.

2. Nieuwhof, "The New Math of Church Plants."

3. Carey Nieuwhof, host, *The Carey Nieuwhof Leadership Podcast*, episode 600, "Jim Davis on The Great Dechurching, The Fastest and Largest Church Attendance Exit in U.S. History, and the $24 Billion in Giving that Left the Church," September 28, 2023.

4. Nieuwhof, "Jim Davis on The Great De-churching."

5. Nieuwhof, "The New Math of Church Plants."

6. Nieuwhof, "The New Math of Church Plants."

Phase Three: Share Faith

1 . Planning Center Online (PCO) is just one of many organizational systems churches can use to develop groups and serving opportunities. It's popular and comprehensive.

KEEP GOING

You reached the last page. The work is not over.
The best part starts now.

Scan the code below for the online tools I built to walk with you as you rebuild worship. Put them to work this week. You will find:

- Short videos from me to set the vision and name what gets in the way
- A quick self-check for your team
- Sample charts to print and work through
- A guide for working through this book with your team
- Stories from real churches who have done this work

Bring these to your launch team. Work through them together. Come back when you need them again, because you will.

Scan to begin.

https://bit.ly/rebuilding-extras

www.ingramcontent.com/pod-product-compliance
Lightning Source LLC
LaVergne TN
LVHW080539130726
843114LV00004B/4

* 9 7 8 1 7 9 1 0 4 2 1 1 0 *